Farm *to* Fork

Also by Emeril Lagasse

· ·

EMERIL 20-40-60: FRESH FOOD FAST

EMERIL AT THE GRILL: A COOKBOOK FOR ALL SEASONS

EMERIL'S CREOLE CHRISTMAS

EMERIL'S DELMONICO: A RESTAURANT WITH A PAST

EMERIL'S NEW NEW ORLEANS COOKING

EMERIL'S POTLUCK: COMFORT FOOD WITH A KICKED-UP ATTITUDE

EMERIL'S THERE'S A CHEF IN MY SOUP!: RECIPES FOR THE KID IN EVERYONE

EMERIL'S THERE'S A CHEF IN MY FAMILY!: RECIPES TO GET EVERYBODY COOKING

EMERIL'S THERE'S A CHEF IN MY WORLD!: RECIPES THAT TAKE YOU PLACES

EMERIL'S TV DINNERS: KICKIN' IT UP A NOTCH WITH RECIPES
FROM *EMERIL LIVE* AND *ESSENCE OF EMERIL*

EVERY DAY'S A PARTY: LOUISIANA RECIPES FOR CELEBRATING
WITH FAMILY AND FRIENDS

FROM EMERIL'S KITCHENS: FAVORITE RECIPES FROM EMERIL'S RESTAURANTS

LOUISIANA REAL AND RUSTIC

PRIME TIME EMERIL: MORE TV DINNERS FROM AMERICA'S FAVORITE CHEF

Farm *to* Fork

Cooking Local, Cooking Fresh

Emeril Lagasse

With Photography by Steven Freeman

harperstudio
An Imprint of HarperCollins*Publishers*

HarperCollins books may be purchased for educational, business, or sales promotional use. For information please write: Special Markets Department, HarperCollins Publishers, 10 East 53rd Street, New York, NY 10022.

For more information about this book or other books from HarperStudio, visit www.theharperstudio.com.

FIRST EDITION

Designed by Leah Carlson-Stanisic

Library of Congress Cataloging-in-Publication Data

Lagasse, Emeril.
  Farm to fork : cooking local, cooking fresh / Emeril Lagasse ; with photography by Steven Freeman. — 1st ed.
    p. cm.
  ISBN 978-0-06-174295-8
  1. Cookery, American. 2. Farm produce. I. Title.
   TX715.L18245 2010
   641.5973—dc22

                                                       2009052670

10 11 12 13 14   WBC/RRD   10 9 8 7 6 5 4 3 2 1

This book is for all the
farmers and fishermen who
keep on keepin' on. We are
so proud of what you do.

Thank you.

Acknowledgments

The seed of this project has been nurtured along by many folks during the time between planting and harvesting. My heartfelt thanks go out to everyone below for the part they played in helping to bring this book to life:

My family—Alden, EJ, Meril, Jessie, Jillian, Mom, Dad, Mark, Wendi, Katti Lynn, Dolores, Jason, and Jude.

Emeril's Culinary Team: Charlotte Martory, Alain Joseph, Stacey Meyer, Angela Sagabaen, and Kamili Hemphill.

My Homebase team: Eric Linquest, Tony Cruz, Dave McCelvey, Marti Dalton, Chef Chris Wilson, Chef Bernard Carmouche, Chef Dana D'Anzi, Tony Lott, Scott Farber, and George Ditta. And all of the Homebase and Emeril's Restaurant employees.

Photographer Steven Freeman, assistants Kevin Guiler, and Josh Maready, and prop stylist Jen Lover.

My Martha Stewart Living Omnimedia associates—Martha, Charles, Robin, Lucinda, and the MSLO test kitchen staff.

Mimi Rice Henken and TJ Pitre.

Michelle Terrebonne and Maggie McCabe.

HarperStudio: Bob Miller, Debbie Stier, Jessica Wiener, Julia Cheiffetz, Katie Salisbury, Kathryn Ratcliffe-Lee, Mary Schuck, Leah Carlson-Stanisic, Kim Lewis, Lorie Young, Nikki Cutler, Doug Jones, Andrea Rosen, Kathie Ness, and Ann Cahn.

Carrie Bachman.

Partners: All-Clad, T-Fal, and Wusthof.

Friends: Leonard Simchick Prime Meats and Fresh Poultry, Pisacane Fish Market, Claggett Farms, Ben and Ben Becnel's, Nunez Seafood, Frank and Richard Santorsola, Sherif, Jim Griffin, and Mark Stein.

Contents

leafy greens

the three sisters: corn, beans, and squash

nightshades

berries, figs, and melons

the orchard

cole crops: broccoli, cabbage, and cauliflower

thistles, stalks, and pods

roots, shoots, tubers, and bulbs

winter fruits

home economics: preserving the harvest

Introduction

I HAVE HAD A CONNECTION WITH THE SOIL SINCE I WAS A YOUNG BOY.

This was kindled long ago, when Dad and I would visit my Uncle Oliver's farm in Westport, Massachusetts. I really looked up to Uncle Oliver, who made his living by growing and baling hay and raising hogs, chickens, goats, sheep, as well as growing fruits and vegetables. I remember being very happy walking the strawberry rows in spring—Uncle Oliver allowed me to pick to my heart's content. I was also encouraged to help in the harvesting of beans, peppers, zucchini, cucumbers—you name it—and then looked forward to every fall for the arrival of cole crops, potatoes, and the magic of pumpkins.

This must have inspired Dad, too, because not much later he converted a good acre-plus of our backyard in Fall River into a vegetable garden, which we tended together. What we didn't eat or share with friends and family was put into my little red wagon and peddled around the neighborhood, particularly to Gene's Market, just a couple blocks from home.

As I got older, I began to take part in the milking of cows and goats and collecting eggs from the chicken coop. It was this experience that really taught me how a farm works. I made the connection between the food we buy at the market and the people who grow it,

and that really stuck with me. Once I became a chef and began honing my craft, I knew the most important thing was to use the freshest and the best ingredients I could find. I also recognized that those ingredients, whether they be seafood, meat, poultry, or produce, should be grown and harvested locally.

A lesson from an early age of what makes great food.

By 1983, when I came to Louisiana and was given a chance to make a name for myself at Commander's Palace in New Orleans, local ingredients were what I relied upon and how I became inspired. It was during those early years as a chef that I, along with a few other chefs and a great farmer, started a farm co-op in nearby Mississippi. The result was fresh produce and herbs straight from the farm and the beginning of "hog Wednesdays." On that day, our farmer would bring freshly slaughtered pigs to the restaurant, and we used every part in every which way—a tradition that remains at Emeril's Restaurant in New Orleans to this day. We took great pride in the fact that everything we made was completely from scratch: from goat cheese to ice cream, from Worcestershire sauce to house-cured bacon. And twenty years later, the focus remains the same for me: fresh quality ingredients make for good food and an exceptional quality of life. My passion for fresh farm-grown ingredients continues to grow stronger. All of the chefs who work in each of my restaurants around the country carry on the tradition of using the freshest ingredients and of maintaining long-lasting connections with local farmers. It is this principle that has inspired the recipes you'll find in these pages: recipes that rely on simple techniques to really allow the integrity of the food to shine through.

"Buy fresh, Buy local" is a slogan that both my restaurants and my family try to live by—and a very important message that I feel compelled to pass along to folks as I encounter them in my travels each day. I try to instill this in my kids by bringing them with me when I shop for family meals. Not only is it fun for them to help Dad pick out the produce, but they also get a lesson in forging relationships with the people who work hard to provide it. It is also the perfect time to speak to them about why it's important to . . .

Support your local farmer's markets.

With the constraints placed on farmers in this country, we really do owe it to ourselves and to them to give our support. If you can, try to find farmers who take the harder road and grow organically—your family's health, not to mention a better ecosystem and a lighter carbon footprint, will be your reward. With more than 4,500 farmer's markets nationwide, and more popping up every day, there is really no reason not to support our local markets. The vendors are able to showcase the very best of what is in season locally—small dairies sell milk, cream, and cheese from cows living perhaps only a few miles away, and farmers bring in produce that heralds the arrival of each season. How exciting it is to see these products on our tables, picked at the peak of ripeness and full of nutrients and vitality. It doesn't get much better than this. An added bonus is that there is no excess packaging to recycle, and no annoying little stickers to pry off your fragile produce. Also, small farmers often grow different and unusual, often heirloom, varieties of produce that many of us have not seen in our lifetimes but which probably graced the tables of the family that went before us.

Our local farmer's markets often support not only farmers but also the men and women who brave the local waters to bring us freshly caught fish, shrimp, crabs, oysters, and a host of other treasures. There has been much in the news lately (but not nearly enough) about the hard times these folks are having competing with the low prices of seafood imported from China and other countries. I know firsthand that Gulf Coast shrimpers are really hurting in this regard; the prices that they are offered at the docks don't even cover their operating costs. Families who have been fishing and shrimping for generations are now being forced to find different livelihoods. If we want to continue to enjoy the wonderful seafood that these people work hard to bring to us, then we must make different choices about where we purchase our seafood. Simple as that.

The way I see it, it's returning to a way of life that used to be taken for granted. Buy locally and you are able to enjoy the benefits that come along with it. Plant a small garden in your backyard, or even just an herb garden in pots on a windowsill. Either way, talk about a great way to spend time with the family! And hey, finicky children are much more likely to try a new vegetable if they've taken part in growing it. The wonder of planting a seedling, watching it grow, and harvesting it to eat is inexplicable. I can't think of a better way to show a child the value of fresh food from the table.

Some of us living in urban environments may not feel we have the opportunities for gardening and farming at home, and may feel unconnected to the sources of our food. But urban farms are popping up in the most unlikely places, such as the still struggling post-Katrina 9th ward of New Orleans. Previously blighted properties are now hosting thriving gardens, where abandoned car tires find new life as containers for vertical potato gardening. (Yes, I've seen it!) New Orleans is home to many such urban farms these days, and these projects not only bring life into neglected parts of town but also enrich the local communities by giving neighbors a reason to come together and work toward a common goal. I know this is happening across the nation, and the message I'm getting to is this: there is a limit only if we allow ourselves to imagine one.

I have been inspired by seeing folks tackle this challenge head-on in unique ways. For instance, the Edible Schoolyard project founded in California by Alice Waters, the head of the buy local, eat fresh movement, has had a tremendous impact on the children involved as well as on the

local community in which the project was founded. I was so impressed by this project that I have worked with Alice and some other folks in order to bring an edible schoolyard to one of our schools in New Orleans. As a result, children are eating better, more healthful meals, and have a genuine respect for Mother Earth and the hard work required to put food on the table. They are learning about nutrition, gardening, and the impact of farming on our environment. All this, plus they're gaining the self-esteem that comes from self-reliance. Visiting these children and seeing what they are learning in the garden, and the smiles on their faces after a day spent in their teaching kitchen, is some very powerful medicine, let me tell you. The pride in what they've accomplished goes farther than the schoolyard, too. The surrounding community comes together to help the children maintain the garden. Neighbors meet and greet and go home feeling that they've done something worthwhile with their time. It's a win-win situation. Just imagine the impact this could generate if we had more programs like this around the country.

And that's what I'm talking about, folks: a connection. It really can be about the choices we make. We can have more to say about what we eat. From the garden, to you, to the table. Go on, make some friends.

Farm to Fork

the herb garden

A LESSON IN HERB OILS: CHIVE, BASIL, MINT

One of the best ways to preserve the abundance of fresh herbs from your garden is by making flavored oils. Herb oils can be enjoyed so many ways— drizzled over salads, vegetables, pastas, sandwiches, or grilled items, hot or cold or in between. Not only are they flavorful, but they also add dramatic color when drizzled on plates. If you want to kick it up, and I know you do, add half a clove of smashed garlic and ⅛ teaspoon crushed red pepper to the blender with the other ingredients . . . a great dipping oil for chunks of rustic bread!

BASIL OIL

3 cups water

2 ounces fresh basil leaves (about 2 cups packed)

¾ cup canola, grapeseed, or other vegetable oil

⅛ teaspoon salt

1. In a small bowl, combine 1 cup ice cubes with 1 cup of the water. Set it aside.

2. Bring the remaining 2 cups water to a boil in a small saucepan. Add the basil leaves all at once, stirring to make sure they are submerged, and cook for 10 seconds. Immediately transfer them, using a slotted spoon, to the ice bath. Once they have cooled, remove the basil leaves and set them on paper towels. Squeeze the paper towels gently but firmly in your hands to absorb as much liquid as possible, and set aside.

3. Pour the oil and salt into a blender, and mix on high speed. While the machine is running, add half the basil leaves and process briefly. Then add the remaining basil and puree it (doing this in batches prevents bruising the leaves and keeps the color intact). Transfer the basil oil to a small container, cover, and refrigerate for up to 1 week. (If you like, strain the oil through a fine-mesh sieve.)

1 cup

CHIVE OIL

4 cups water

2 ounces (about 2 bunches) fresh chives, snipped to 3-inch lengths (2 cups)

¾ cup canola, grapeseed, or other vegetable oil

⅛ teaspoon salt

1. In a small bowl, combine 1 cup ice cubes with 1 cup of the water. Set it aside.

2. Bring the remaining 3 cups water to a boil in a small saucepan. Add the chives all at once, stirring to make sure they are submerged, and cook for 10 seconds. Immediately transfer them, using a slotted spoon, to the ice bath. Once they have cooled, remove the chives and set them on paper towels. Squeeze the paper towels gently but firmly in your hands to absorb as much liquid as possible.

3. Combine the chives, oil, and salt in a blender and mix on high speed for 1½ to 2 minutes, until thoroughly combined. Transfer the Chive Oil to a small container, cover, and refrigerate for up to 1 week. (If you like, strain the Chive Oil through a fine-mesh sieve.)

1 cup

MINT OIL

4 cups water

2 ounces fresh mint leaves (about 2 cups packed)

¾ cup canola, grapeseed, or other vegetable oil

⅛ teaspoon salt

1. In a small bowl, combine 1 cup ice cubes with 1 cup of the water. Set it aside.

2. Bring the remaining 3 cups water to a boil in a small saucepan. Add the mint leaves all at once, stirring to make sure they are submerged, and cook for 10 seconds. Immediately transfer them, using a slotted spoon, to the ice bath. Once they have cooled, remove the mint leaves and set them on paper towels.

Squeeze the paper towels gently but firmly in your hands to absorb as much liquid as possible.

3. Combine the mint leaves, oil, and salt in a blender and mix on high speed for 1½ to 2 minutes, until thoroughly combined. Transfer the mint oil to a small container, cover, and refrigerate for up to 1 week. (If you like, strain the mint oil through a fine-mesh sieve.)

1 cup

FRESH MINT TEA

Is the garden overgrown with mint? No problem! This recipe is adapted from the traditional Moroccan mint tea, where green tea is used instead of black, but still with an abundance of fresh spearmint. It is enjoyed there throughout the day—so why not here too?

4 cups water

1½ cups loosely packed fresh
    spearmint leaves

⅓ cup sugar

Two ¼-inch-thick orange slices
    (do not peel)

6 whole cloves

2 orange pekoe tea bags

1. Bring the water to a boil in a saucepan.

2. In another saucepan, combine the spearmint leaves, sugar, orange slices, cloves, and tea bags. Carefully pour the boiling water over the tea mixture, and let it steep for 3 minutes. Stir to dissolve the sugar, and then strain the tea into a small warmed teapot or other serving vessel. Serve hot.

1 quart, 2 to 4 servings

CHEESY HERBED POPOVERS

It's hard not to stare at the oven while these bake, and rise, and pop. The aroma alone will get 'em out of bed to come see the action. By no means do you want to open the oven until the popovers are finished. Don't worry—you won't ruin their gorgeous color. Leave them in until the last moment to be sure the inside is cooked.

4 tablespoons (½ stick) butter, melted

½ cup grated Parmigiano-Reggiano cheese

4 eggs

1 teaspoon salt

½ teaspoon freshly ground black pepper

1½ cups whole milk

3 tablespoons heavy cream

1 cup all-purpose flour

2 tablespoons chopped mixed fresh herbs, such as parsley, thyme, rosemary, basil, or chives

About 2 ounces medium cheddar cheese, grated (½ cup) or cut into 12 pieces

1. Preheat the oven to 450°F.

2. Brush the cups of a standard 12-cup muffin tin with some of the melted butter. Divide the Parmesan evenly among the cups.

3. Combine the eggs, salt, pepper, milk, cream, and the remaining butter in a blender and blend until well combined. Add the flour and blend for 15 seconds, until smooth. Transfer the batter to a large mixing bowl. Stir in the fresh herbs.

4. Fill each muffin cup halfway with batter. Divide the cheddar among the cups, and then top with the remaining batter.

5. Bake the popovers for 15 minutes. Then reduce the heat to 350°F and bake for 10 minutes.

6. Remove the muffin tin from the oven and unmold the popovers onto a wire rack. Pierce the side of each popover with a small sharp knife to allow steam to escape. (This will help keep them from deflating.) Serve immediately.

12 popovers, 6 to 8 servings

CILANTRO PESTO

Although cilantro can pack a punch, heat diminishes the flavor of this delicate herb, so making pesto with it is a great way to preserve its bright, clean flavor. Use this pesto as a finish for hot pasta, drizzled on simply cooked meat or fish, or tossed with boiled vegetables. You could even stir it into a pot of beans or soup . . . use it any way in which you'd enjoy traditional basil pesto. This will create added interest to any dish.

2 cups packed fresh cilantro leaves

¾ cup hulled pepitas (raw pumpkin seeds), toasted

½ cup grated Cotija cheese

2 cloves garlic, crushed

1 cup plus 2 tablespoons canola, grapeseed, or other neutral oil

1 teaspoon grated lime zest

2 tablespoons freshly squeezed lime juice

1¼ teaspoons salt

½ teaspoon freshly ground black pepper

1. Place the cilantro, pepitas, Cotija, and garlic in a food processor and blend until just smooth. With the motor running, add the oil in a slow, steady stream. Transfer the mixture to a bowl, and stir in the lime zest, juice, salt, and pepper.

2. Use immediately, or refrigerate for up to 2 days, or store the pesto in an airtight container in the freezer for up to 1 month.

Generous 1½ cups

HERBED GOAT CHEESE BUTTONS

These serve as a wonderful spread for crackers or crusty bread, and they make a nice addition to a cheese plate or a simple green salad.

. . . .

11 ounces soft, mild goat cheese, at room temperature

2 tablespoons minced fresh basil leaves

1 tablespoon minced fresh oregano leaves

½ teaspoon minced fresh rosemary or thyme leaves

1½ teaspoons minced garlic

1 to 2 tablespoons extra-virgin olive oil, plus more for serving

Kosher salt and freshly ground black pepper

Fresh herb sprigs, for lining the serving platter (optional)

1. In a small bowl, combine the goat cheese, basil, oregano, rosemary, garlic, and 1 tablespoon of the olive oil. Stir until well combined. If the mixture is too stiff to mix well, add the remaining oil, a little at a time, and stir to combine. Season with kosher salt and black pepper to taste. Cover the mixture and place in the refrigerator to stiffen, 30 minutes to 1 hour. (This will make it easier to roll.)

2. Use a small spoon or scoop to portion the cheese mixture into roughly 2-tablespoon portions. Lightly oil your hands to prevent sticking, and use them to roll each portion into a small ball; then lightly flatten it to form a "button." Place the buttons on a platter (lined with herb sprigs if desired), and refrigerate it, lightly covered with plastic wrap, until ready to serve, up to 1 week.

3. Allow the buttons to come to room temperature. Then drizzle them with olive oil as desired, and serve.

About 13 buttons

HERB SALAD

In this salad herbs are used like lettuce, courtesy of your garden or your neighborhood farmer's market. Large pieces are tossed with red leaf, a lemony bright vinaigrette, chopped eggs, and capers. Any leftover vinaigrette is delicious over steamed green beans or grilled fish.

3 tablespoons 1-inch-long snipped chives

3 tablespoons fresh parsley leaves

3 tablespoons fresh mint or tarragon leaves

3 tablespoons roughly chopped fresh basil leaves

1½ tablespoons minced shallot

1½ teaspoons finely grated lemon zest

2 tablespoons freshly squeezed lemon juice

4 tablespoons canola or other vegetable oil

2 tablespoons extra-virgin olive oil

Salt and freshly ground black pepper

One 12-ounce head red or green leaf lettuce, or a mix, rinsed and spun dry, and torn into bite-size pieces

2 hard-boiled eggs, chopped

2 tablespoons nonpareil capers, drained

2 tablespoons finely grated ricotta salata

1. Combine all the herbs (there should be a generous ¾ cup total) and set aside in a small bowl.

2. In another bowl, add the shallot, lemon zest, and lemon juice. Slowly whisk in both oils to form a vinaigrette. Add ½ teaspoon salt and ¼ teaspoon pepper, and set aside.

3. Combine the lettuce, herbs, eggs, and capers in a medium bowl. Season lightly with salt and pepper. Stir the vinaigrette and add 4 tablespoons. Toss gently. Divide the salad among six serving plates or transfer it to a serving bowl. Garnish with the cheese, and drizzle with more vinaigrette as desired.

6 servings

HERB-CRUSTED HALIBUT

The herb crust provides a zesty crunch that brightens up a halibut fillet. The simplicity of this dish makes it perfect for a weeknight dinner and yet still sophisticated enough for weekend entertaining. If you cannot find halibut at your local fish market, substitute another mild, flaky white fish.

4 teaspoons chopped lemon zest

4 teaspoons chopped fresh dill leaves

4 teaspoons chopped fresh parsley leaves

4 teaspoons chopped fresh chervil leaves

2 teaspoons cracked black pepper

Four 6-ounce halibut fillets, skinned

1½ teaspoons salt

4 teaspoons Dijon mustard

1 tablespoon vegetable oil

4 cups fresh arugula leaves, rinsed and spun dry

2 tablespoons olive oil

1. In a shallow bowl, combine the lemon zest, dill, parsley, chervil, and black pepper.

2. Season the fish with 1¼ teaspoons of the salt. Then lightly brush one side of each fillet with 1 teaspoon of the Dijon mustard. Firmly press the mustard-coated side of each fillet into the lemon-herb mixture.

3. Heat the vegetable oil in a skillet (preferably non-stick). Place the fillets, coated side down, in the hot oil and cook until the crust turns golden, 3 to 3½ minutes. Flip them over and continue to cook until the fish flakes easily, about 3 minutes.

4. Meanwhile, toss the arugula with the olive oil in a medium bowl, and season with the remaining ¼ teaspoon salt. Divide the arugula evenly among four serving plates.

5. Place a halibut fillet on each mound of arugula, and serve immediately.

4 servings

OPAL BASIL-MACERATED PEACHES

Did you know there are at least twenty-five varieties of basil, coming in all shapes, sizes, flavors, and scents? Basil is actually a member of the mint family, making it useful in both sweet and savory dishes. Opal basil is similar in flavor to sweet basil, but I chose opal basil for this dish because I just love the color of its deep purple leaves. Basil lends an unexpected flavor to this simple dessert.

4 firm-ripe peaches, peeled, pitted, and quartered

1 ounce opal basil leaves (about 2 cups loosely packed)

1 teaspoon grated lime zest

1 cup sugar

1 cup water

Homemade Crème Fraîche, for serving (page 134, optional)

1. Place the peaches and basil in a medium bowl, and set it aside.

2. Combine the lime zest, sugar, and water in a medium saucepan. Bring to a boil, stirring to dissolve the sugar. Lower the heat and simmer for 2 minutes. Then pour the hot syrup over the peaches and basil. Cover, and chill for 2 hours.

3. Serve the peaches in small bowls, garnished with a dollop of crème fraîche if desired.

4 to 6 servings

ROSEMARY BUTTERMILK SCONES

These are not the old-tasting dried-out scones you may have had. They are flaky and wonderful. The aroma of orange and rosemary from your oven . . . ahhh. Enjoy them with fresh creamery butter, clotted cream, or the Orange Curd on page 195.

3 cups all-purpose flour

1 tablespoon sugar

1 tablespoon baking powder

½ teaspoon baking soda

1 teaspoon salt

¼ teaspoon freshly ground black pepper

½ teaspoon finely grated orange zest

1 tablespoon chopped fresh rosemary leaves

12 tablespoons (1½ sticks) cold unsalted butter, cut into pieces

1 cup plus 2 tablespoons well-shaken buttermilk

1. Preheat the oven to 425°F. Line a baking sheet with parchment paper, and set it aside.

2. In a medium bowl, sift together the flour, sugar, baking powder, baking soda, salt, and black pepper. Add the orange zest and rosemary, and combine with a fork. Add the butter and work it into the flour with your fingers, a pastry blender, or a fork until the mixture resembles coarse crumbs. (A few large flat pieces of flour-coated butter in the mixture are okay—they'll contribute to the flakiness.)

3. Add the 1 cup buttermilk and stir with a fork until the ingredients are just moistened. Gather the dough together and press it gently into a rough ball. Turn the dough out onto a lightly floured surface and pat it together (with floured hands, if necessary). The dough

may still be a crumbly mass. Knead the dough gently six to seven times; then use your hands to shape it into a rectangle measuring about 7 by 4 inches. With a lightly floured rolling pin, roll the dough into a 10½ × 7-inch rectangle, ¾ inch thick. Use a knife to divide the dough into three sections by cutting it at roughly 3¼-inch intervals along the length. Cut each rectangle in half. You will have 6 squares. Cut each square into 2 triangles.

4. Set the triangles on the prepared baking sheet, and brush them with the remaining 2 tablespoons buttermilk. Bake for 12 to 14 minutes, until golden brown and puffed. Serve warm.

12 scones

WELSH-STYLE CHEESE TOAST

The traditional name for this toast is Welsh Rabbit or Welsh Rarebit. It has a long history and is steeped in quite a bit of lore. According to some, when the hunter came home without a rabbit, his wife would make this sandwich instead—the melting cheese combined with a little ale would just have to do. Today we're more than happy to eat this delicious tidbit as a snack. Using good-quality whole-grain bread and the best-quality cheese is the key to making this dish delicious.

1 pound cheese, such as Vella Monterey Jack, cheddar, Fontina, or a combination of cheeses, grated

½ cup beer

1 large egg, lightly beaten

1 teaspoon Worcestershire sauce

1 teaspoon Dijon mustard

1 teaspoon salt

¼ teaspoon sweet pimentón (smoked Spanish paprika) or sweet paprika

4 strips crisp-cooked bacon, crumbled

6 slices whole-grain bread, toasted

6 slices beefsteak tomato

1. Combine the cheese and the beer in the top of a double boiler set over boiling water. Warm the cheese gently until it melts. Then add the egg, Worcestershire, mustard, salt, pimentón, and bacon, and stir to combine. Cook for 2 minutes, and remove from the heat.

2. Preheat the broiler. Line a baking sheet with aluminum foil.

3. Arrange the toast on the prepared baking sheet, and top each piece with a slice of tomato. Ladle the cheese mixture over the top. Broil until the cheese is bubbling and golden brown, about 2 minutes.

4. Serve immediately.

6 servings

FARMER'S MARKET FRITTATA

Breakfast, brunch, lunch, or dinner? And anywhere in between: eat a frittata. You can easily substitute other chopped vegetables, cup for cup, for the filling ingredients here. You could also use leftover cooked ingredients such as potatoes, kale, or spinach: chop them small and warm them in the pan with the other ingredients just before you add the eggs.

8 eggs

3 tablespoons heavy cream

½ teaspoon salt

¼ teaspoon freshly ground black pepper

3 tablespoons butter

1 cup thinly sliced onions

1 cup thinly sliced yellow, red, or orange bell peppers, or a mix

1 cup thinly sliced mushrooms (about 4 ounces)

1 cup fresh corn kernels

1 cup diced smoked ham

2 tablespoons chopped fresh herbs, such as chives, basil, thyme, parsley, oregano, or your favorite mixture

1 cup grated Swiss cheese (about 4 ounces)

1. Set a rack in the upper third of the oven and pre-heat the broiler.

2. In a small bowl, whisk the eggs, cream, salt, and pepper together until combined.

3. Melt 2 tablespoons of the butter in a 10-inch oven-proof sauté pan over medium-high heat. Add the onions and peppers and cook, stirring as needed, until soft, 7 to 8 minutes. Add the mushrooms and corn and cook for 2 minutes. Add the ham and cook until warmed through, 1 minute. Add the remaining 1 tablespoon butter, and when it has melted, add the egg mixture. Sprinkle the fresh herbs over the eggs, and top with the grated cheese. Reduce the heat to medium and cook the eggs, undisturbed, for 3 minutes, or until the surface begins to bubble and the bottom starts to set.

4. Immediately place the sauté pan in the oven and broil until golden brown on top, 3 to 4 minutes.

5. Remove the pan from the oven. Using a rubber spatula, loosen the frittata from the sides of the pan. Tilt the pan and gently slide the frittata onto a platter. Serve hot or warm.

6 servings

HERBED QUICHE WITH BLUE CHEESE

This quiche is a perfect creamy balance of blue cheese, cream, and fresh herbs baked in a pastry shell. Believe me, it's luscious. Enjoy this alone or accompanied with a salad and a nice glass of white wine. Who said "real men don't eat quiche"? This will show who's da man.

1 Savory Pie Crust (page 83)

6 ounces cream cheese, at room temperature

2 ounces Maytag blue cheese, at room temperature

2 tablespoons unsalted butter, at room temperature

3 eggs

1 cup heavy cream

1 cup whole milk

½ teaspoon salt

¼ teaspoon freshly ground black pepper

3 tablespoons chopped fresh mixed herbs, such as parsley, thyme, tarragon, chives, and/or oregano

1. Preheat the oven to 400°F.

2. On a lightly floured surface, roll out the pie crust dough to ⅛-inch thickness to fit an 8-inch fluted tart pan. Fill the pan with the dough, easing the dough into the bottom and lightly pressing it against the sides. Trim off the excess dough.

3. Line the pastry shell with parchment paper, and fill it with ceramic pie weights or dried beans. Place the tart pan on a baking sheet, and bake for 9 minutes. Remove the baking sheet from the oven and set the tart pan on a wire rack to cool. Remove the parchment paper and the weights.

4. Reduce the oven temperature to 375°F.

5. In a medium bowl, whisk together the cream cheese, blue cheese, and butter. Whisk in the eggs until well blended. Stir in the cream, milk, salt, pepper, and herbs. Pour the filling into the partially baked pie shell. Return the tart pan to the baking sheet and bake, rotating the quiche halfway through, until it is puffed and golden brown, 25 minutes. The quiche is done when a knife inserted in the center comes out clean.

6. Remove the tart pan from the baking sheet and set it on a wire rack to cool for at least 5 minutes before slicing. Serve hot, warm, or at room temperature.

6 to 8 servings

SHIRRED EGGS

These eggs are so delicious and easy—a wonderful dish to serve at a small brunch get-together. Just be sure to watch them carefully toward the end of the baking time so that the yolks are cooked just to your liking.

1 teaspoon butter

4 thin slices Virginia or Black Forest ham (about ½ ounce each)

8 eggs, at room temperature

Salt and freshly ground black pepper

4 tablespoons heavy cream

1 teaspoon chopped fresh parsley leaves

1 teaspoon chopped fresh tarragon leaves

1 teaspoon chopped fresh chives

½ cup grated Swiss cheese

1. Preheat the oven to 325°F.

2. Butter four shallow 6-ounce baking dishes, and lay 1 slice of ham in each so that it sits flat on the bottom (it's okay if it comes up the sides). Crack 2 eggs into a small bowl, and then transfer the eggs to one of the dishes so that the eggs sit side by side on top of the ham. Season the eggs lightly with salt and pepper. Repeat with the remaining eggs. Add 1 tablespoon cream to each dish. Place the filled dishes on a baking sheet, and bake until the eggs are just beginning to set and the whites are opaque, about 10 minutes.

3. Remove the baking sheet from the oven. Top each dish with a sprinkling of the fresh herbs and 2 tablespoons of the cheese. Return the baking sheet to the oven and cook until the eggs are the desired doneness, 7 to 10 minutes. Serve immediately.

4 servings

FRESH RICOTTA

Soft cheeses such as ricotta, fromage blanc, and mozzarella are the best choices for beginning cheesemakers because they are so easy to make at home. Try to find fresh milk from a local farmer. If that is not available, be sure to purchase organic milk from your grocer.

1 gallon milk

1 teaspoon citric acid (see Notes)

1 teaspoon cheese salt or non-iodized plain salt (see Notes)

1. Pour the milk into a stainless-steel or other nonreactive pot. Add the citric acid and salt, and stir. Heat the milk to 195°F, stirring constantly to avoid scorching.

2. When the curds and whey separate, remove the pot from the heat and let it sit for 5 minutes.

3. Line a colander with cheesecloth. Ladle the curds gently into the cloth. Tie the cloth to form a bag, and hang it to drain for at least 30 minutes. (Depending on the desired consistency, the cheese could be drained for a longer period of time.)

4. Once it has drained to the desired consistency, the cheese is finished and ready to eat. You can store the cheese in an airtight container in the refrigerator for up to 2 weeks.

About 2 quarts

Notes: Citric acid is a white powder obtained from the juice of citrus and/or other acidic fruits. It is most commonly used as a flavoring agent, but is also used to aid in coagulation when making soft cheeses. Citric acid is usually available from cheese-making supply houses.

Cheese salt is similar to pickling salt and is made of noniodized coarse flakes. Iodine inhibits the growth of starter bacteria and slows the aging process, so using a salt containing iodine would be counterproductive when making cheese. Cheese salt can usually be found from cheese-making supply houses, but if you cannot find it in your area, a good substitute is Diamond Crystal Kosher Salt.

HOMEMADE MOZZARELLA

Make sure that you use milk that is not ultra-pasteurized for this recipe, because that process alters the protein in the milk and it will not work properly. Milk from a small creamery is best, as most major brands are likely to be ultra-pasteurized.

¼ rennet tablet, or ¼ teaspoon liquid rennet (see Note)

1¼ cups cool distilled water

1½ teaspoons citric acid (see Notes, page 23)

1 gallon whole milk (not ultra-pasteurized)

¾ teaspoon cheese salt or non-iodized plain salt

1. In a small bowl or cup, stir the rennet into ¼ cup of the water. Set it aside.

2. Combine the citric acid with the remaining 1 cup water in another small bowl, and stir until it has dissolved.

3. Pour the milk into a large stainless-steel or other nonreactive pot, and stir vigorously while adding the citric acid solution. Set the pot over medium heat, and heat the milk to 90°F, stirring continuously with a large spoon.

4. Remove the pot from the heat and slowly stir in the rennet solution. Use the large spoon to stir with an up-and-down motion, so that you are bringing the curd from the bottom of the pot to the top, for approximately 30 seconds. Then cover the pot and leave it undisturbed for 5 minutes.

5. Check the curd: it should look like custard, with a clear separation between the curd and the whey. If the curd is too soft or the whey is too milky, let it sit for a few more minutes. Then roughly cut the curd, using a long knife that reaches to the bottom of the pot, into large dice.

6. Return the pot to the heat, and heat the mixture to 110°F while slowly moving the curds around with your spoon. Then remove it from the heat and continue to stir slowly for 2 to 5 minutes (the longer the stirring, the firmer the cheese).

7. Heat a large pot of water to 185°F. Fill a large bowl with ice and cold water, and set it aside.

8. Line a heatproof colander with cheesecloth, and ladle the curds into it. Fold the curds gently as you drain off the whey. Let the curds sit for a minute. Then remove and discard the cheesecloth, sliding the curds into the colander. Dip the colander, with the curds in it, into the hot water. Do this several times. Then take a spoon and fold the curds until they start to become elastic and stretchable, 30 seconds to 1 minute. When it is stretchable, remove the curd from the liquid and pull it like taffy. (This stretching elongates the proteins.) If it does not stretch easily, return it to the hot water for more heat.

9. At this point, add the salt and work it into the cheese. Stretch the cheese until it is smooth and shiny. You can now form the cheese into a log, ball, or bite-size morsels. When you're finished, submerge the cheese in ice water and leave it for 10 minutes. (This cools it down and allows the cheese to hold its shape, protecting the silky texture and keeping it from becoming grainy.) Drain, wrap in plastic wrap, and refrigerate for up to 2 weeks.

12 ounces

Note: Rennet is a substance that contains enzymes that act on the milk protein, casein, creating coagulation. This causes the milk curds (solids) to separate from the whey (liquid). Rennet can come in liquid, tablet, or powdered form and is usually available from cheese-making supply houses as well as in some health food stores.

CROSTINI WITH RICOTTA AND SPRING PEAS

Spring peas, with their vibrant green hue and sweet flavor, are perfect on their own and best when picked fresh off the vine. If you happen to come across fresh peas at your farmer's market, look for peas that are plump, bright green with no visible germ. Peas have a high sugar content, which quickly turns to starch, so they are best when eaten shortly after being harvested. In this recipe, sweet peas are paired with fresh ricotta cheese and a little Parmesan. The delicate flavors are well matched for a light snack or as a starter for a spring brunch.

1½ cups spring peas

1 baguette or other crusty bread

¼ cup olive oil

Salt and freshly ground black pepper

2 teaspoons minced garlic

14 ounces fresh ricotta cheese, store-bought or homemade (see page 23)

3 tablespoons extra-virgin olive oil, plus more for drizzling

1 tablespoon plus 1 teaspoon chopped fresh mint leaves

1 tablespoon minced shallot

2 tablespoons finely grated Parmigiano-Reggiano cheese

1 teaspoon chopped fresh basil leaves

1. Fill a medium bowl with ice and cold water, and set it aside.

2. Bring a saucepan of salted water to a boil over high heat. Add the peas and cook until the water returns to a boil. Drain, and immediately submerge the peas in the ice water. When they have cooled, drain them again and set them aside.

3. Preheat an outdoor grill or a grill pan to medium-high.

4. Slice the baguette into 3-inch-long oval slices, ¼ inch thick. Brush one side of each slice with the olive oil, and season them with ⅛ teaspoon salt and ⅛ teaspoon pepper. Grill on both sides until toasted. Set aside.

5. On a cutting board, sprinkle ¼ teaspoon salt over 1 teaspoon of the minced garlic. Chop the garlic and mash it with the flat side of your knife until the mixture forms a paste. In a small bowl, combine the garlic paste, ricotta, 1 tablespoon of the extra-virgin olive oil, the 1 tablespoon mint, the shallot, and ½ teaspoon pepper. Mix well, and set aside.

6. In another small bowl, mash the spring peas with the back of a fork until there are no whole peas; you should have a mixture of pea halves and paste. Add ⅛ teaspoon salt, ⅛ teaspoon pepper, 1 teaspoon minced garlic, 2 tablespoons extra-virgin olive oil, the 1 teaspoon mint, and the Parmesan and basil. Stir gently to combine.

7. Spoon about 1 tablespoon of the ricotta mixture onto each crostini, and spoon about 2 teaspoons of the pea mixture on top of the ricotta mixture. Repeat with the remaining crostini. Drizzle extra-virgin olive oil over the top as desired, and serve.

24 crostini, about 6 servings

HONEY VANILLA GOAT'S MILK ICE

Fresh goat's milk has a tangy and slightly grassy taste that is truly unique. Goat's milk is gaining popularity across the United States as we are becoming more aware of the array of high-end products, such as cheese and yogurt, made by artisanal producers. If possible, use goat's milk from a local goat farmer for this recipe. Taste the difference!

3 cups goat's milk

2 whole vanilla beans, split
    lengthwise

½ cup honey

4 eggs

1. In a large, heavy-bottomed saucepan, gently heat the milk with the vanilla beans and honey. Once the milk is hot, remove the pan from the heat and set it aside for 5 to 10 minutes to allow the vanilla to infuse. Then remove the vanilla beans, and discard them or set them aside for another purpose. Set the hot milk aside.

2. Using an electric mixer, beat the eggs until lemon-yellow, about 4 minutes. Little by little, add the milk to the eggs, whisking constantly to prevent the eggs from curdling. Strain the mixture through a fine-mesh sieve into a bowl, and refrigerate, covered, until it is thoroughly chilled, at least 2 hours and up to overnight.

3. Freeze the ice milk in an ice cream maker according to the manufacturer's directions.

1 quart

BUTTERMILK CANDY

As with the fudge (page 33), you have to watch the temperature carefully here: make sure you cook the candy to 240°F. If you don't cook it long enough, it will simply be a delicious sauce. But done right, the result is a caramelized, milky-flavored confection that you simply will not be able to resist.

2 cups buttermilk

2 teaspoons baking soda

¼ cup light corn syrup

4 cups sugar

8 tablespoons (1 stick) unsalted butter, at room temperature

2 teaspoons vanilla extract

1. Butter an 8×8-inch baking dish, and set it aside.

2. Combine the buttermilk and baking soda in a 6-quart (or larger) heavy-bottomed pot (the mixture will bubble a lot while cooking, so you need a large pot to keep it from boiling over). Let it stand for 20 minutes.

3. Add the corn syrup and sugar to the buttermilk, and stir well. Attach a candy thermometer to the side of the pot. Bring the mixture to a boil over medium heat. Then reduce the heat to low and simmer until it reaches 240°F (soft-ball stage; see the headnote on page 33). The mixture will become caramelized and dark brown in color. While it cooks, stir it intermittently to keep it from bubbling over, and adjust the heat as necessary. This will take about 1¼ hours.

4. Remove the pot from the heat and set it aside. Leave it, undisturbed, until the mixture cools to 120°F.

5. Add the butter and vanilla to the cooled mixture, and using a handheld electric mixer, beat the mixture on high speed until it loses its gloss and thickens. Pour it into the prepared baking dish, and spread it out evenly. Let it cool completely. Then cut it into 1-inch pieces.

About 64 pieces

EMERIL'S ANYTIME EGGNOG

You don't have to wait until December to enjoy eggnog—and you don't have to have a party, either. Think of it as a delicious after-dinner drink or a dessert, any time of the year! The most wonderful eggs, milk, and cream are available at your farmer's market year-round—I gotcha there. The eggnog can be bottled, corked, and refrigerated for several days—the flavor will be even better. Shake before serving.

12 eggs, separated (see Notes)

1¾ cups sugar

6 cups whole milk

1 vanilla bean, split lengthwise

⅛ teaspoon salt

¾ cup good-quality bourbon

¾ cup good-quality brandy

¾ cup good-quality dark rum

2 cups heavy cream

Freshly grated nutmeg, for garnish
    (optional)

1. Fill a large wide bowl with ice and cold water, and set it aside.

2. In a medium bowl, whisk the egg yolks with 1 cup of the sugar until the mixture is pale yellow and thick, about 2 minutes.

3. Combine the milk, vanilla bean, and salt in a medium saucepan. Set it over medium heat and bring the mixture to a boil. Remove the pan from the heat. While whisking constantly, slowly drizzle 1 cup of the hot milk into the yolks. Add 1 more cup of the hot milk to the yolks in the same manner. Now that the yolks have been tempered, slowly pour the yolk mixture into the saucepan with the remaining milk while continuing to whisk. Cook over medium heat, stirring constantly with a wooden spoon, for 3 minutes, or until the mixture is thick enough to coat the back of the spoon. Remove the saucepan from the heat.

4. Pour the mixture through a fine-mesh strainer into a large metal bowl set in the ice bath. Stir as needed until cooled, about 20 minutes. Cover the eggnog base, and refrigerate until it is well chilled and ready to use, 1 hour or up to overnight.

5. Place the egg whites (see Note 1) in the bowl of a standing electric mixer fitted with the whisk attachment, and beat until soft peaks form. Slowly add the remaining ¾ cup sugar, beating the whites on high speed until stiff peaks form.

6. Remove the chilled eggnog base from the refrigerator. Whisk in the bourbon, brandy, and rum. Whisk in the heavy cream (see Note 2). Fold in the whipped egg whites, and whisk until the mixture is uniform. Serve immediately, with freshly grated nutmeg if desired, or refrigerate until ready to enjoy.

4 quarts, 8 to 10 servings

Notes: 1. If you prefer to make this eggnog without raw egg whites, eliminate step 5 from the recipe. Instead, whip 3 cups of cream (the 2 cups plus an additional cup) with the ¾ cup sugar until thick, and add this to the eggnog base in step 6. Discard the egg whites or reserve for another use.

2. If you prefer a thicker eggnog, whip the cream before adding it to the eggnog base.

TRIPLE-CHOCOLATE PECAN FUDGE

The secret to getting fudge right is practice and patience. We have given a time range that we recommend you use as an approximation. Really engage your senses and pay attention. Use your thermometer, but another way to gauge the soft-ball stage of the candy is by using an ice bath: When you are ready to test if the fudge has cooked long enough, remove it from the heat and drop a small dollop into the ice bath. After it has cooled for a few seconds, it should form a soft, malleable mass when gripped between your fingertips. This is called the soft-ball stage, and this is what you want for the perfect fudge.

2 ounces unsweetened chocolate, chopped

2 ounces semisweet chocolate, chopped

2 ounces bittersweet chocolate, chopped

1¼ cups half-and-half

3 cups sugar

2 tablespoons light corn syrup

⅛ teaspoon salt

4 tablespoons (½ stick) unsalted butter

1 teaspoon vanilla extract

1 cup pecan pieces (optional)

1. Butter an 8-inch square baking dish, and set it aside.

2. Combine all the chocolate and the half-and-half in a medium saucepan, and warm it over low heat, stirring until the chocolate is completely melted. Add the sugar, corn syrup, and salt, and cook to the soft-ball stage (236° to 240°F), 15 to 20 minutes. Remove the pan from the heat.

3. Add the butter and *do not stir*. Allow the fudge to sit, undisturbed, until it reaches 120°F. Then add the vanilla and the pecans, if using, and beat with a hand-held electric mixer until the fudge loses its gloss and starts to thicken but is still warm enough to pour into the prepared baking dish. The fudge will look less like chocolate sauce and more like chocolate frosting. Spread it out evenly in the dish, and let it cool completely. Then cut it into 1-inch cubes.

64 pieces

leafy greens

LETTUCE SOUP

Most of us think of using lettuce only in salads, but how about cooking it! Butter lettuce and fresh herbs take the starring role in this quick and easy soup. Serve this as the starter to a simple meal any time of the year.

2 tablespoons olive or grapeseed oil

1 large onion, thinly sliced

1 tablespoon minced garlic

1 tablespoon chopped fresh parsley leaves

1 tablespoon chopped fresh chives

1 tablespoon chopped fresh mint leaves

2 teaspoons chopped fresh tarragon leaves

2 heads Boston lettuce, rinsed and coarsely chopped

1 quart chicken stock or canned low-sodium chicken broth

½ cup heavy cream or evaporated milk

1 teaspoon salt

½ teaspoon freshly ground white pepper

1. Heat the olive oil in a large saucepan over medium-low heat. When it is hot, add the onion and garlic and cook until the onion is translucent, about 4 minutes. Add the parsley, chives, mint, tarragon, and lettuce, and stir until the lettuce is completely wilted, about 3 minutes. Add the chicken stock and bring to a simmer. Cook, uncovered, at a low simmer for 20 minutes.

2. Stir in the heavy cream, salt, and pepper, and simmer for another 5 minutes. Allow the soup to cool slightly.

3. Puree the soup, in batches, in a blender (see Note). Pour the pureed soup into a clean saucepan, and warm it gently before serving.

Note: Please use caution when blending hot liquids: blend only small amounts at a time, with the blender tightly covered and a kitchen towel held over the top.

1 generous quart, 4 to 6 servings

BRAISED BLENDED GREENS

Greens begin to pop up in farmer's markets, at roadside stands, and in backyard vegetable gardens when the cool weather arrives—not long after the last tomato has gone. Young greens can be eaten raw in salads and slaws, but heartier greens are best when cooked. Dark leafy greens are chock-full of vitamins and minerals, and I am always trying to find new ways to incorporate them into my diet. Cooking several varieties of greens together provides an assortment of flavors and textures.

4 ounces dandelion greens, stems removed, leaves rinsed, dried, and chopped into bite-size pieces

4 ounces blue kale, stems removed, leaves rinsed, dried, and torn into bite-size pieces

4 ounces Red Russian kale, stems removed, leaves rinsed, dried, and torn into bite-size pieces

4 ounces Lacinato kale, stems removed, leaves rinsed, dried, and torn into bite-size pieces

4 ounces beet greens, stems removed, leaves rinsed, dried, and torn into bite-size pieces

2 tablespoons olive oil

4 ounces hot Italian sausage, removed from casing and crumbled

1 cup sliced yellow onions

1 tablespoon minced garlic

1½ cups chicken stock or canned low-sodium chicken broth

½ teaspoon salt

1. Toss all of the prepared greens together in a large mixing bowl to combine well.

2. Set a deep 12-inch sauté pan over medium-high heat. Add the olive oil to the pan, and once it is hot, add the crumbled sausage. Cook until the sausage is well browned and most of the fat has rendered from it, about 4 minutes.

3. Add the onions to the pan and cook, stirring often until tender, for 3 to 4 minutes. Stir in the garlic and cook for 30 seconds. Add the greens, in batches if necessary, and cook, stirring frequently, until they begin to wilt. Then add the chicken stock and bring it to a simmer. Cook until the greens are tender and most of the liquid has evaporated, 7 to 10 minutes.

4. Stir in the salt, and serve hot.

4 servings

ESCAROLE SOUP

Escarole does have a bitter flavor, but don't turn your back on it just yet. The broth in this soup is delicious, and as it cooks, the escarole actually becomes a little bit sweeter. The soup has a little kick from the crushed red pepper and is rounded out by the cheese. Oh yeah, babe.

2 tablespoons olive oil

2 tablespoons butter

1 large onion, chopped

¼ teaspoon crushed red pepper

10 cloves garlic, minced

8 cups chicken stock or canned low-sodium chicken broth

1 large head escarole (about 10 ounces), rinsed, thick ribs removed, leaves chopped

½ cup finely grated Parmigiano-Reggiano cheese

½ cup finely grated Pecorino Romano cheese

Salt and freshly ground black pepper, to taste

1 tablespoon chopped fresh parsley leaves

1 tablespoon chopped fresh chives

1. In a large saucepan, heat the oil and butter over medium heat. Once the butter has melted, raise the temperature to medium-high and add the onion. Sauté until tender, stirring as needed, about 5 minutes.

2. Add the crushed red pepper and cook for about 1 minute. Add the garlic and cook, stirring constantly to avoid scorching, until it is aromatic, about 1 minute. Add the chicken stock and bring to a boil. Then reduce the heat to a low simmer and cook, uncovered, for about 30 minutes, or until the garlic has mellowed.

3. Add the escarole and simmer until it is tender, about 15 minutes.

4. Meanwhile, stir the Parmesan and Pecorino together in a small bowl.

5. Season the soup to taste with salt and pepper. Add the parsley and chives, and stir to mix well. Ladle the soup into individual bowls, and garnish each bowl with the cheese mixture to taste. Serve hot.

6 servings

CLAGETT FARM SOUTHERN COOKED GREENS

Clagett Farm is a working farm operated by the Chesapeake Bay Foundation in Maryland. Among other things, they grow vegetables for their Community Supported Agriculture program (also known as a CSA), which allows people to prepurchase a share of the harvest. You pay the farmer up front and later the harvest is divided between you and the other "shareholders." In this way they are able to maintain a mutually supportive relationship between farmers and the community. And on top of that, half of the produce they grow on the farm is distributed free or at reduced prices to underserved communities nearby. Talk about sustainability! This recipe is my tribute to the abundance of greens grown on their farm.

2 pounds smoked turkey legs, thighs, or wings

6 cups chicken stock, canned low-sodium chicken broth, or water, or a combination

2 tablespoons canola oil

4 cups thinly sliced onions

1 tablespoon minced garlic

2 teaspoons salt

½ teaspoon crushed red pepper, or 1 or 2 whole dried red peppers, cut in half

6 pounds greens, such as collard, mustard, turnip, or kale, or a mixture, tough ends of the stems removed, leaves rinsed, and chopped into 2- to 3-inch pieces

¼ cup cider vinegar

1. Combine the turkey and broth in a medium pot and bring the broth to a boil. Reduce the heat to low, cover, and simmer for 2 hours, until the turkey is very tender and easily pulls away from the bone. Remove the pot from the heat and set it aside until the turkey is cool enough to handle. Pull the meat from the bones (discard the bones) and return the meat to the broth.

2. Heat the canola oil in a 6-quart pot over medium-high heat. Add the onions and cook, stirring as needed, until translucent, about 6 minutes.

3. Add the garlic, salt, and crushed red pepper, and cook for 1 minute. Add the greens in batches, stirring and pressing them down as they start to wilt to make room for more. When all the greens have been added, add the broth and turkey. Bring to a boil, reduce the heat to low, and simmer for 25 minutes, or until the greens are tender.

4. Stir in the vinegar, and remove from the heat. Remove the pepper halves, if desired. Serve the greens warm with their pot liquor (juices) and turkey.

6 to 8 servings

SPINACH SAUTÉED WITH GARLIC, FIGS, AND HONEY

Sweet and savory come together nicely in this dish that is just an explosion of flavors. You may have to sauté the spinach in batches; whatever you do, just work quickly so you don't overcook it.

2 tablespoons olive oil

2 tablespoons thinly sliced garlic

¼ cup sliced dried figs

¼ cup chicken stock or canned low-sodium chicken broth

1 pound baby spinach, rinsed and spun dry

½ teaspoon salt

¼ teaspoon freshly ground black pepper

2 teaspoons honey

1. Place a medium skillet over medium-high heat. Add the olive oil, and when it is hot, add the garlic and cook until it is lightly toasted, about 30 seconds. Add the figs and chicken stock, and cook until the stock is nearly completely reduced, 1 to 2 minutes. Add the spinach and cook, stirring, until wilted, about 2 minutes.

2. Season with the salt and pepper, and drizzle with the honey just before serving.

4 servings

SWISS CHARD BOULES FILLED WITH LEMON BARLEY "RISOTTO"

This elegant dish takes about two hours to make but is very impressive: an almost vegetarian cabbage roll, if you will (it can be made with vegetable stock and without the pancetta). If you don't want to pull out all the stops and make the whole dish, the lemon barley risotto can be made without the chard stems and enjoyed on its own. It is especially delicious drizzled with the Mint Oil on page 3.

1 pound Swiss chard, with at least 12 large leaves (it is easier to make the boules with large leaves)

3 tablespoons butter

2 ounces pancetta, diced

¼ cup diced shallot

¾ cup pearled barley

1 teaspoon kosher salt

½ teaspoon freshly ground white or black pepper

¼ cup dry white wine

3¼ cups chicken, beef, or vegetable stock or canned low-sodium chicken, beef, or vegetable broth, heated

¼ cup plus 2 tablespoons finely grated Parmigiano-Reggiano cheese

¼ cup chopped fresh parsley leaves

1 teaspoon finely grated lemon zest

Roasted Red Pepper Coulis (recipe follows)

1. Fill a large bowl with ice and cold water, and set it aside.

2. Bring a large pot of salted water to a boil, add the Swiss chard, and cook until the leaves are pliable enough for rolling, 1½ minutes. Immediately transfer the chard to the bowl of ice water, and let it cool for 2 minutes. Drain, and lay the chard on clean kitchen towels to dry. Pat dry.

3. Cut the large ribs and stems from the center of the chard leaves, and set the leaves aside. Finely dice the ribs and stems, and reserve them separately. You should have about 1 cup of diced ribs/stems.

4. Place a medium saucepan over medium-high heat. Add the butter and the pancetta, and cook until the pancetta begins to crisp, about 2 minutes. Add the shallot and reserved diced chard stems and ribs, and cook until tender, 3 to 4 minutes. Add the barley, salt, and pepper, and cook for 1 minute. Add the white wine and cook, stirring, until it has evaporated. Then begin adding the chicken stock in ½-cup increments, stirring constantly and adding more stock when each first addition has been completely absorbed. Continue this process until you have used 3 cups of the stock; this will take about 40 minutes. Then fold in the cheese, parsley, and lemon zest, and adjust the seasoning if necessary. Set the "risotto" aside until it is cool enough to handle. (The "risotto" will cool faster if you spread it on a small parchment-lined baking sheet and chill it in the freezer for 10 minutes.)

5. Preheat the oven to 300°F.

6. Using a 2-ounce scoop or a ¼-cup measure and your hands, form the barley "risotto" into approximately 12 round balls. Place each ball at the bottom edge of the inside of a Swiss chard leaf. Roll the ball up in the leaf, tucking the edges in and rotating the ball so that the barley is evenly covered and the edges of the leaf are smooth. Repeat with the remaining barley "risotto" balls and Swiss chard leaves. You should be able to form about 12 boules. If your leaves are torn or are small, you can still make boules by piecing a few leaves together.

7. Arrange the boules in a shallow baking dish and add the remaining ¼ cup stock. Cover the dish with aluminum foil and bake for 30 minutes, or until the boules are completely warmed through. Serve immediately, drizzled with the Roasted Red Pepper Coulis.

12 boules, 4 to 6 servings

ROASTED RED PEPPER COULIS

1 pound (about 3) red bell peppers, roasted, skins and seeds removed

¼ cup pine nuts, toasted

2 tablespoons red wine vinegar

½ cup finely grated Parmigiano-Reggiano cheese

1 tablespoon chopped fresh parsley leaves

1 tablespoon chopped fresh basil leaves

1 tablespoon freshly squeezed lemon juice

¼ cup extra-virgin olive oil

½ teaspoon salt

¼ teaspoon freshly ground white pepper

Combine all the ingredients in the bowl of a food processor and process to form a thick, creamy puree. Adjust the seasoning, if necessary.

2 cups

To Roast Peppers and Chiles

1. Set the peppers directly over the flame of a gas burner set on high, and cook, in batches and turning as necessary, until blackened on all sides, about 6 minutes. (See Note.) Transfer the peppers to a bowl and cover it with plastic wrap, allowing them to steam.

2. Once the peppers are cool enough to handle, remove and discard the stems, the skin, and most of the seeds (by just running your fingers over the pepper). Use as desired.

Note: If you don't have a gas stove, you can roast peppers in the oven: Toss them in 1 teaspoon oil, place them on a baking sheet, and roast at 450°F until blackened on all sides, turning them as necessary.

DANDELION GREENS WITH WALNUTS, BLUE CHEESE, AND DATES

Dandelion greens fall into the category of bitter greens and can be rather strong on their own. However, their hearty texture and sharp flavor make a great backdrop when paired with a sweet date dressing, salty cheese, and toasted walnuts.

1 teaspoon minced shallot

¼ teaspoon Dijon mustard

2 tablespoons water, or as needed

3 tablespoons balsamic vinegar

3 whole dried pitted dates, plus ¼ cup finely diced

¼ teaspoon salt, plus more to taste

⅛ teaspoon freshly ground black pepper, plus more to taste

6 tablespoons grapeseed oil

4 cups chopped dandelion greens (bite-size pieces)

4 ounces Rogue River or other blue cheese, crumbled

½ cup chopped toasted walnuts

1. Combine the shallot, mustard, water, balsamic vinegar, and the 3 whole dates in a food processor or blender, and blend together well. Season with the ¼ teaspoon salt and ⅛ teaspoon black pepper, and continue to blend while adding the oil in a slow, steady stream until the vinaigrette is smooth and emulsified. Transfer the vinaigrette to a small bowl and stir in the chopped dates.

2. Place the dandelion greens in a large mixing bowl, and add 3 tablespoons of the vinaigrette. Season with a pinch of salt and pepper (or to taste), and toss to coat well. Divide the greens among four serving plates, and sprinkle the blue cheese and walnuts over them. Drizzle with additional vinaigrette, making sure each dish gets enough date pieces. Serve immediately.

About 4 servings

FRISÉE AND ARUGULA SALAD WITH PAN-FRIED OYSTERS AND CREAMY FENNEL DRESSING

Freshly shucked local oysters are one of the great pleasures that come from living close to the water. You know how to enjoy them on the half-shell. Here they are pan-fried and crown fresh peppery greens.

. . . .

4 ounces sliced bacon, cut into ½-inch strips

1 bulb fennel (about 1 pound), halved and cored

Salt

2 tablespoons olive oil

⅓ cup finely diced shallot

1 teaspoon minced garlic

1 teaspoon freshly ground white pepper

⅓ cup Herbsaint or Pernod liqueur

1 egg yolk

3 tablespoons water

1 tablespoon freshly squeezed lemon juice

1½ cups canola, grapeseed, or other vegetable oil

1 cup yellow cornmeal

1 teaspoon freshly ground black pepper

¼ teaspoon cayenne pepper

12 medium-size shucked oysters (about 8 ounces)

8 cups (about 10 ounces) fresh arugula or spinach, large stems removed, leaves rinsed and spun dry

1 small head frisée, rinsed, core removed, leaves pulled apart (about 2 cups)

¼ cup freshly grated Parmigiano-Reggiano cheese

1 apple, cored and thinly sliced or julienned

1. Cook the bacon in a small sauté pan over medium-high heat until it is crispy, 7 to 9 minutes. Drain, and set the bacon aside on paper towels to cool. Crumble the cooled bacon, and set it aside.

2. Thinly slice one half of the fennel bulb on a mandoline, or with a sharp knife, and set it in a small bowl. Sprinkle with ½ teaspoon salt and set it aside for 20 minutes. Then rinse the fennel well under cool water, pat it dry, and cover and refrigerate until ready to use.

3. Cut the remaining fennel into small dice. Heat the olive oil in a 10-inch sauté pan over medium-high heat. Add the diced fennel, shallot, garlic, ½ teaspoon salt, and ½ teaspoon of the white pepper. Cook until tender, stirring as necessary, about 3 minutes. Carefully add the Herbsaint to the pan and cook until the liquid has been absorbed, 2 minutes. Remove the pan from the heat and set it aside to cool for 5 minutes.

4. Combine the egg yolk, water, lemon juice, ½ teaspoon salt, the remaining ½ teaspoon white pepper, and the sautéed fennel in the bowl of a food processor. Process until smooth. While the machine is still running, add 1 cup of the canola oil in a thin, steady stream until incorporated. Transfer the dressing to a small container, cover, and refrigerate. (If desired, the dressing can be thinned to your liking with additional water.)

5. In a shallow pan, stir together the cornmeal, 2 teaspoons salt, the black pepper, and the cayenne. Dredge each oyster in the cornmeal mixture and set them aside.

6. Heat the remaining ½ cup vegetable oil in a 12-inch sauté pan over medium-high heat. Add the oysters and cook until they are golden and the centers are set, 1½ to 2 minutes per side. Drain on paper towels.

7. To assemble the salad, combine the arugula, frisée, reserved sliced fennel, reserved bacon, Parmesan, and apple in a large mixing bowl. Add ¼ cup of the dressing (or more if desired), and toss gently to combine. Divide the salad among four to six serving plates. Divide the oysters among the salads, and serve immediately.

4 to 6 servings

WILTED CHARD WITH WALNUT PESTO AND A BALSAMIC REDUCTION

With rainbow chard, you get the beautiful hues of pink, gold, red, and white stems mixed with glossy green leaves all in one bunch. Ah, the glories of nature. If you can't find rainbow chard, this recipe is still wonderful with any local variety.

2 cups packed flat-leaf parsley leaves

¾ cup chopped toasted walnuts

½ cup grated Parmigiano-Reggiano cheese

2 cloves garlic, crushed

1 cup extra-virgin olive oil

2 tablespoons freshly squeezed lemon juice

1 teaspoon grated lemon zest

1½ teaspoons salt

½ teaspoon freshly ground black pepper

½ cup balsamic vinegar

2 tablespoons grapeseed or olive oil

3 bunches rainbow chard, ribs removed, leaves rinsed and julienned

1. Place the parsley, walnuts, Parmesan, and garlic in the bowl of a food processor or blender, and process until finely chopped. With the motor running, slowly add the olive oil in a thin stream through the feed tube and process until it forms a paste. Remove the top and scrape down the sides of the bowl. Add the lemon juice, zest, ¾ teaspoon of the salt, and ¼ teaspoon of the pepper. Transfer the walnut pesto to a bowl and set it aside.

2. Pour the balsamic vinegar into a small saucepan, and cook over medium-high heat until it is reduced by half, 6 to 7 minutes. Transfer the balsamic reduction to a small bowl and set it aside.

3. In a large sauté pan, heat the grapeseed oil over medium-high heat. When it is hot, add the chard, the remaining ¾ teaspoon salt, the remaining ¼ teaspoon pepper, and 3 tablespoons of the walnut pesto. Toss the chard with the pesto to coat and warm through, 2 to 3 minutes.

4. Transfer the chard to a serving platter, drizzle with the balsamic reduction, and serve immediately.

4 servings

the three sisters: corn, beans, and squash

CORN OYSTERS

These fritters, though made entirely of corn, resemble fried oysters—hence their name. They are traditional summer fare, made with fresh-shucked corn straight from the field. When corn is plentiful at the market, get as much as you can and enjoy it every which way.

4 ears fresh corn

2 eggs, separated

2 tablespoons heavy cream

2 tablespoons minced jalapeño

1 cup all-purpose flour

2 teaspoons baking powder

1¼ teaspoons salt

½ teaspoon cayenne pepper

Pinch of sugar

Vegetable oil, for frying

Emeril's Original Essence or other
　　Creole seasoning, for garnish

1. Holding the base of an ear of corn in a medium bowl, slice downward, cutting halfway through the kernels. Using the back of the knife or a small spoon, scrape downward along the cob to extract the milk, letting it fall into the bowl with the cut kernels. Cut again along the cob, this time cutting close enough to remove the remaining half of the kernels. Repeat with the remaining ears.

2. In a small bowl, whisk the egg yolks until pale and slightly thickened, about 2 minutes. Then add the yolks to the corn. Stir in the heavy cream and jalapeño.

3. Stir the flour, baking powder, salt, cayenne, and sugar together in a bowl. Then stir the flour mixture into the corn mixture until just combined. Do not overmix.

4. Beat the egg whites until medium to stiff peaks form. Fold the whites into the corn mixture until thoroughly combined.

5. Fill a heavy-bottomed Dutch oven or a deep iron skillet halfway with vegetable oil (so it is 2 to 4 inches deep). Heat the oil over medium-high heat until it reaches 350°F.

6. When the oil is hot, carefully add 2-tablespoon scoops of the corn mixture, working in batches and being careful not to overcrowd the pan. (While they are cooking, the fritters may spatter hot oil, so be careful; a splatter screen may come in handy.) Fry the fritters for 6 minutes, or until they are golden and cooked through, turning them as needed for even color. Remove, and drain on a paper towel–lined plate. Season with the Essence, and serve immediately.

24 fritters, 4 to 6 servings

TEMPURA SQUASH BLOSSOMS

These can be eaten alone as a fun light snack or appetizer. Or try them as a garnish on top of salads.

Gather the fragile blossoms in the morning, before they've had a chance to wilt in the midday sun. Wrap them in lightly dampened paper towels and then place them in plastic food storage bags; refrigerate until you're ready to fry 'em up.

Vegetable oil, for deep-frying (see Note)

⅔ cup all-purpose flour

½ cup cornstarch

½ teaspoon salt, plus more for seasoning

¼ teaspoon cayenne pepper

1 large egg, beaten

1 cup cold seltzer water

20 fresh squash blossoms

1. Heat the oil in a deep-fryer to 360°F.

2. In a mixing bowl, whisk together the flour, cornstarch, the ½ teaspoon salt, and the cayenne. Add the egg and seltzer water, and mix well to make a smooth batter, being careful to not overwork it.

3. Dip each blossom into the batter, and then shake it to remove any excess. Carefully add the blossoms to the hot oil, working in batches so as not to overcrowd the fryer, and fry until crispy, 3 to 4 minutes. Transfer the blossoms to paper towels to drain.

4. Season the blossoms lightly with salt, and serve immediately.

Note: If you do not own a deep-fryer, see step 5 on page 50 for instructions on frying in a Dutch oven. Make sure to keep the temperature of the oil as close to 360°F as possible.

20 squash blossoms, about 4 servings

ROASTED BUTTERNUT SQUASH SOUP

As butternut squash ripens, the inside turns deep orange and its flavor becomes sweeter and richer. Roasting large chunks, instead of whole halves, gives more tasty caramelized edges from a cranked-up oven.

4 pounds butternut squash, peeled, seeded, and cut into 3-inch chunks

¼ cup olive oil

1 tablespoon salt

1 teaspoon freshly ground black or white pepper

3 tablespoons butter

3 cups chopped onions

½ cup chopped carrots

1 clove garlic, smashed

1 or 2 sprigs fresh thyme

1 cup brandy

4 cups chicken stock or canned low-sodium chicken broth, plus more if needed

4 cups water

Homemade Crème Fraîche, for garnish (page 134, optional)

Herb oil of choice, for garnish (see pages 2 and 3, optional)

1. Preheat the oven to 450°F. Line a rimmed baking sheet with parchment paper.

2. Place the cut squash in a large bowl and toss with the olive oil, 1 teaspoon of the salt, and ½ teaspoon of the pepper. Transfer the squash to the prepared baking sheet and roast in the oven for 25 minutes, or until the squash is lightly caramelized and tender. Remove it from the oven and set aside.

3. While the squash is roasting, melt the butter in a 6-quart pot over medium heat. Add the onions, carrots, garlic, thyme, 2 teaspoons salt, and ½ teaspoon pepper. Cook until the vegetables are soft, about 10 minutes. Add the brandy, cook for 5 minutes, and then add the stock and water. Bring to a boil, reduce the heat, and simmer for 15 minutes.

4. Add the roasted squash to the pot, and remove it from the heat. Discard the thyme sprigs.

5. Blend the soup using an immersion blender, or in several batches in a blender until it is completely smooth. Transfer the blended soup to a decorative soup pot or to individual serving bowls. Serve hot, garnished with a dollop of crème fraîche and a drizzle of herb oil if desired.

3 quarts, 8 to 10 servings

Note: Please use caution when blending hot liquids: blend only small amounts at a time, with the blender carefully covered and a kitchen towel held over the top.

CORN, TOMATO, AND LOBSTER SALAD

The freshest corn is so delicious that you don't need to bother cooking it. Simply toss the kernels with vinaigrette, tiny heirloom tomatoes, and steamed lobster. What's not to love? It's no question.

2 cups roughly chopped ripe tomatoes

2 cups dry white wine

½ cup water

1 cup thinly sliced onions

3 black peppercorns

2 sprigs fresh tarragon

One 1½-pound lobster

2 tablespoons minced shallot or red onions

2 tablespoons champagne vinegar or white wine vinegar

2 tablespoons freshly squeezed lemon juice

½ teaspoon grated lemon zest

⅓ cup plus ½ teaspoon extra-virgin olive oil

½ teaspoon salt, plus more for seasoning

⅛ teaspoon cayenne pepper

1¼ cups Silver Queen (or other regional variety) fresh corn kernels (from about 2 ears)

1 pint mixed tiny heirloom tomatoes, such as cherry, cherub, grape, or pear, of different colors and sizes

2 tablespoons chopped fresh tarragon leaves

1 tablespoon chopped fresh parsley leaves

8 Bibb lettuce leaves, rinsed and patted dry

Freshly ground black pepper

1. Fill a large bowl with ice and cold water, and set it aside.

2. In a 4- or 6-quart Dutch oven, or other heavy-bottomed pot with a tight-fitting lid, combine the chopped tomatoes, wine, water, onions, peppercorns, and tarragon sprigs. Bring to a boil over high heat, uncovered; then reduce the heat to a simmer and cook for 15 minutes.

3. Raise the heat to high, add the lobster to the pot, and cover the pot immediately with a heavy, tight-fitting lid. Steam the lobster for 13 minutes, until it is bright red and the long feelers are easily removed from their sockets. Immediately plunge the lobster into the bowl of ice water, and let it cool for 5 minutes.

4. Remove the lobster from the ice water and set it on a rimmed baking sheet. Using kitchen shears, remove the lobster meat from the tail and claws. Use a knife to chop the lobster meat into bite-size pieces. You should have about 1 cup; set it aside.

5. In a medium nonreactive mixing bowl, combine the shallot, vinegar, lemon juice, and lemon zest. Whisk in the ⅓ cup extra-virgin olive oil, ½ teaspoon salt, and the cayenne. Add the corn kernels and mix together. Set aside for 10 minutes.

6. Cut the tiniest heirloom tomatoes in half, and quarter the larger ones. Add the tomatoes to the corn mixture. Add the lobster, tarragon, and parsley, and mix gently to combine.

7. In a medium bowl, gently mix the Bibb lettuce leaves with the remaining ½ teaspoon extra-virgin olive oil, and season them lightly with salt and black pepper. Stack 2 lettuce leaves on each of four plates. Divide the lobster salad evenly among the lettuce cups, and serve immediately.

4 servings

BABY LIMAS, GREEN AND YELLOW BEANS, AND TEARDROP TOMATOES WITH MINT VINAIGRETTE

This simple, beautiful salad is all about fresh, fresh, fresh. Try to get young, tender beans and fresh baby limas for the best results, and don't overcook them; the texture should be crisp-tender. If you feel like making this when fresh limas are unavailable, simply substitute an equal amount of frozen baby lima beans or edamame.

2 tablespoons minced shallot

⅓ cup rice vinegar

⅓ cup chopped fresh mint leaves

⅓ cup grapeseed, flaxseed, or olive oil

1½ teaspoons sugar

¼ cup salt, plus more for seasoning

8 ounces yellow wax beans, ends trimmed

8 ounces green beans, ends trimmed

2 cups fresh baby lima beans

1 pint red and yellow teardrop tomatoes (or other cherry-size tomatoes), cut in half lengthwise

2 tablespoons chopped fresh lemon basil leaves

2 tablespoons chopped fresh cilantro leaves

Freshly ground black pepper, to taste

1. Combine the shallot, rice vinegar, mint, oil, and sugar in a small bowl. Set it aside.

2. Fill a large bowl with ice and cold water, and set it aside.

3. Bring a large pot of water to a boil. Add the ¼ cup salt, and stir to combine. Then add the yellow wax and green beans, and cook until the beans are crisp-tender, about 4 minutes. Using a slotted spoon, transfer the beans to the ice bath (leave the boiling water on the heat). When the beans are cool enough to handle, remove them from the ice bath and drain well. Toss the beans with 2 tablespoons of the vinaigrette in a medium bowl.

4. Add the lima beans to the boiling water and cook until tender, about 2 minutes. Drain, and place the beans in the ice bath. When they have cooled, remove them from the ice bath and drain well.

5. In a large salad bowl, combine the wax beans, green beans, lima beans, tomatoes, and the remaining vinaigrette. Add the lemon basil and cilantro, and toss gently to combine. Season with salt and freshly ground black pepper to taste, and serve.

4 to 6 servings

CHARRED CHAYOTE SOUP WITH ADOBO SHRIMP

This simple soup contains a lot more depth and flavor than meets the eye. Don't skip grilling the chayote—it adds a smoky element that really makes this combination sing.

2½ pounds chayote squash (2 to 3 squash), peeled, halved, and seeded

1 tablespoon vegetable oil

1¼ teaspoons salt

¼ teaspoon freshly ground black pepper

1 pound medium shrimp, peeled and deveined

2 teaspoons adobo sauce from canned chipotles in adobo sauce

2 tablespoons unsalted butter

½ cup diced onions

1 teaspoon minced garlic

½ teaspoon ground cumin

¼ teaspoon crushed red pepper

1 quart chicken stock or canned low-sodium chicken broth

1 tablespoon finely chopped fresh cilantro leaves

Sour cream, for garnish (optional)

1. Preheat a grill or grill pan to medium-high heat.

2. In a large bowl, toss the chayote with the vegetable oil, ½ teaspoon of the salt, and the black pepper. Place the chayote on the grill and cook, in batches if necessary, until it is slightly charred on both sides, 8 to 10 minutes per side. Remove from the heat, cut into ½-inch dice, and set aside.

3. Toss the shrimp, ¼ teaspoon of the salt, and the adobo sauce together in a bowl, and let stand for at least 10 and up to 30 minutes.

4. Heat the butter in a medium stockpot or soup pot over medium-high heat. Add the onions and the remaining ½ teaspoon salt, and cook until they have softened, about 3 minutes. Add the garlic and cook, stirring, for 30 seconds. Add the reserved chayote, the cumin, and the crushed red pepper. Stir in the chicken stock and bring the mixture to a boil. Then reduce the heat to medium-low and simmer until the chayote is tender, about 8 minutes.

5. Add the shrimp and cook for 2 minutes, or until they are cooked through. Remove the soup from the heat and stir in the cilantro. Serve the soup immediately, garnished with sour cream if desired.

About 2 quarts, 4 to 6 servings

TOASTED GARLIC ROMANO BEANS

Don't skimp on the amount of garlic here—it's what makes this simple dish so remarkable. If you cannot find romano beans in your area, you could certainly substitute blanched green beans here without a hitch.

1½ pounds romano beans

¼ cup extra-virgin olive oil

⅓ cup thinly sliced garlic

1 cup halved cherry or grape tomatoes

1 teaspoon minced fresh thyme leaves

1 teaspoon minced fresh rosemary leaves

1 teaspoon minced fresh oregano leaves

1 teaspoon kosher salt

½ teaspoon freshly ground black pepper

½ cup chicken stock or canned low-sodium chicken broth

1. Fill a medium bowl with ice and cold water, and set it aside.

2. Bring a large saucepan of lightly salted water to a boil. Add the romano beans and cook them until crisp-tender, 2 to 4 minutes. Then immediately drain the beans and submerge them in the ice bath. When they are cool enough to handle, drain them well. Trim the ends and cut the beans into 2-inch lengths on the diagonal. Set them aside.

3. Heat half of the olive oil in a large skillet over medium-high heat. Add the garlic and cook, stirring, until lightly toasted, 1 to 2 minutes. Add the remaining oil and the tomatoes, thyme, rosemary, oregano, salt, and pepper. Cook, stirring frequently, until the tomatoes have softened slightly, about 2 minutes. Add the stock and the romano beans, and cook, stirring, until the beans are heated through and well coated with the garlic and tomatoes, 2 to 3 minutes. Serve immediately.

6 servings

LEMON-SCENTED ORECCHIETTE PASTA WITH FAVA BEANS AND FRESH TARRAGON

Fresh fava beans make their debut in the spring. With their outer pod and inner protective skin, these legumes may seem formidable, but I assure you they are worth the effort. Fresh fava beans have a nutty, creamy flavor that is often paired with tender herbs. The combination of lemon and tarragon provides an aromatic background for the beans, enhancing their natural sweetness.

2 cups shelled fava beans

8 ounces orecchiette pasta

3 tablespoons extra-virgin olive oil

½ cup minced shallot or ramps

1 tablespoon minced garlic

½ cup dry white wine

1 cup chicken stock or canned low-sodium chicken broth

½ teaspoon finely grated lemon zest

3 tablespoons butter

2 teaspoons minced fresh tarragon leaves

1¼ teaspoons salt, plus more if needed

½ teaspoon freshly ground black pepper, plus more if needed

½ cup finely grated Parmigiano-Reggiano cheese, plus more for garnish if desired

1. Fill a medium bowl with ice and cold water, and set it aside.

2. Bring a large saucepan of lightly salted water to a boil. Add the shelled fava beans and cook them until just tender, 3 to 4 minutes. Then immediately drain the beans and submerge them in the ice bath. When they are cool enough to handle, drain them well. A bean at a time, pinch off a strip of the skin and pop the bean out of the skin into a bowl. Set it aside.

3. Bring a large pot of salted water to a boil, and add the orecchiette.

4. While the orecchiette are cooking, make the pasta sauce: Heat the olive oil in a large skillet over medium-high heat. Add the shallot and sauté until soft, about 2 minutes. Add the garlic and cook until fragrant, 1 to 2 minutes. Add the white wine and cook until it is nearly completely reduced, 2 to 3 minutes. Add the chicken stock and cook until it has reduced by half, 2 to 3 minutes. Then add the favas, lemon zest, butter, tarragon, salt, and pepper, and cook until the favas are heated through and the sauce is thick and flavorful. Remove the skillet from the heat.

5. When the pasta is al dente (after about 10 minutes), drain it in a colander. Add the pasta to the skillet, return the skillet to the heat, and cook, stirring, until the pasta is coated with the sauce. Add the ½ cup Parmesan and toss to combine. Taste, and re-season if necessary. Serve immediately, garnished with additional Parmesan if desired.

4 appetizer servings

ROASTED SPAGHETTI SQUASH WITH PARMESAN CURLS

This is a simple preparation for the magical spaghetti squash. I still think, "Oooh . . ." when I shred it into "noodles" with a fork. Enhance this dish with one of the Herb Oils on page 2, or serve it with fresh tomato sauce.

2 spaghetti squash (about 5 pounds total)

4 tablespoons olive oil

1 teaspoon salt

½ teaspoon freshly ground black or white pepper

3 tablespoons butter, at room temperature

2 tablespoons chopped fresh herbs, such as chives, parsley, thyme, or a mix

2 ounces Parmigiano-Reggiano cheese, shaved with a vegetable peeler (about ½ cup)

1. Preheat the oven to 400°F. Line a baking sheet with parchment paper.

2. Slice the spaghetti squash in half lengthwise, and scoop out the seeds. Drizzle the cut side of each half with 1 tablespoon of the olive oil, and season with the salt and pepper. Place the squash, cut sides down, on the prepared baking sheet. Bake for 45 minutes to 1 hour, or until the squash is tender when pierced with the tip of a knife.

3. Remove the squash from the oven and set them aside until they are cool enough to handle. Then, shred the interior of the squash with a fork (it will resemble strands of spaghetti), placing the "noodles" in a bowl. Add the butter and fresh herbs, and toss to combine. Divide the squash among six serving plates, top with the curls of Parmesan, and serve warm.

6 servings

BRAISED PINTO BEANS

Sweet paprika and jalapeño make the flavors in this dish complex and fiery, yet subtle. Just the way you should enhance fresh beans: nothing more, and I wouldn't give you anything less. If you're afraid of the heat, simply remove the seeds from the jalapeño before mincing it.

Serve these in bowls or ladled over rice.

4 ounces sliced applewood-smoked bacon, cut into ½-inch pieces

1 cup diced onions (small dice)

1 teaspoon minced garlic

¼ cup finely chopped fresh cilantro stems

1 medium jalapeño, minced (about 2½ tablespoons)

½ teaspoon sweet paprika

½ teaspoon salt

1 pound fresh pinto beans

4 cups chicken stock or canned low-sodium chicken broth

1 tablespoon chopped fresh cilantro leaves

1 tablespoon chopped fresh oregano leaves

1. Cook the bacon in a 3- to 4-quart pot over medium heat until it is crispy and the fat is rendered, 5 to 7 minutes.

2. Add the onions, garlic, cilantro stems, jalapeño, paprika, and salt, and cook, stirring occasionally, until the onions are soft, 3 minutes.

3. Add the beans and the chicken stock, and bring to a boil. Then reduce the heat to low and simmer, uncovered and stirring occasionally, for 1 hour, or until the beans are tender.

4. Remove the pot from the heat, and stir in the chopped cilantro and oregano. Serve warm.

About 1 quart, 2 to 4 servings

PATTYPAN SQUASH WITH BACON, CARAMELIZED ONIONS, AND CHEDDAR

This simple, Southern-inspired dish relies on young, tender pattypan squash. Make sure you get small pattypans because they will have the tenderest skins, and cook them only until they are crisp-tender for the best texture. For you vegetarians out there, this is equally delicious without the bacon: simply sauté the onions in 3 tablespoons butter in place of the rendered bacon fat.

4 quarts water

3 pounds young pattypan squash

6 ounces sliced smoked bacon

2 medium onions, diced

¼ cup plus ¾ teaspoon salt

½ teaspoon freshly ground black pepper

1 tablespoon minced fresh thyme leaves

2 tablespoons unsalted butter

8 ounces medium cheddar cheese, grated (about 2 cups)

1. Preheat the oven to 350°F. Pour the water into a large stockpot or soup pot, and place it over high heat.

2. While waiting for the water to boil, trim the root and stem ends from the squash, and then cut each squash in half crosswise. Cut each half into ½-inch-thick wedges. Set them aside.

3. Cook the bacon in an ovenproof 4- or 5-quart straight-sided sauté pan over medium-high heat until it is crisp, 4 to 6 minutes. Transfer the bacon to paper towels to drain, and set aside.

4. Add the onions to the hot bacon fat and cook, stirring frequently, until they are soft and caramelized around the edges, about 6 minutes. Season with the ¾ teaspoon salt and the pepper. Add the thyme and the butter, stir to combine, and set the sauté pan aside.

5. Add the remaining ¼ cup salt to the boiling water, and stir to combine. Add the squash to the boiling water and cook, stirring occasionally, until it is crisp-tender, about 6 minutes. Drain in a colander, shaking to remove as much water as possible, and then add the squash to the sautéed onions and toss gently to combine. Crumble the cooked bacon over the squash, and

then top with the cheese. Cover the pan with aluminum foil, place it in the oven, and bake until the
cheese is melted and the squash is hot throughout,
about 10 minutes. Serve immediately.

6 to 8 servings

PROVENÇAL-STYLE STUFFED ZUCCHINI

Any gorgeous variety of zucchini from the market can work in this recipe. One day you may find the cylindrical shape; another, the round shape. I've tried both. And who doesn't love stuffed zucchini? We bake these until the zucchini is nicely cooked through. If you need the crumbs to brown a little more, fire up the broiler for a minute at the end.

2 cups (about 2 ounces) diced French baguette or other crusty bread, preferably day-old (½-inch dice)

½ cup finely grated Parmigiano-Reggiano cheese

¼ cup packed fresh parsley leaves

1 tablespoon minced garlic

½ teaspoon salt, plus more if needed

¼ teaspoon freshly ground black pepper, plus more if needed

3 tablespoons extra-virgin olive oil

8 small zucchini (each about 7 inches long and 1¼ to 1½ inches wide)

4 ounces fresh lean mild pork sausage

¾ cup minced onions

1 cup finely chopped peeled and seeded tomatoes (about 2 medium tomatoes)

1. Pulse the diced bread in a food processor until you have an even mix of fine and coarse crumbs. Add ¼ cup of the Parmesan, the parsley leaves, 1½ teaspoons of the minced garlic, ¼ teaspoon of the salt, and ⅛ teaspoon of the pepper, and process until evenly mixed. Reserve 2 tablespoons of the breadcrumb mixture for the filling. Mix 1½ tablespoons of the extra-virgin olive oil into the remaining breadcrumbs, transfer the mixture to a small container, and set it aside. (Alternatively, you can use store-bought fine fresh crumbs: Combine ¾ cup breadcrumbs with 1 tablespoon minced parsley, ½ teaspoon minced garlic, ¼ cup finely grated Parmesan, ¾ teaspoon salt, and ⅛ teaspoon freshly ground black pepper. Set aside 2 tablespoons, and mix 1½ tablespoons extra-virgin olive oil into the remainder.)

2. Lay the zucchini on a flat work surface, and using a sharp knife, slice off the top quarter of each squash lengthwise. Next, slice a sliver off the bottom of each squash to help keep it stable. Using a small melon baller or spoon, remove the inner flesh from the zucchini to form a small boat shape, leaving a shell that is approximately ¼ inch thick. Cut the zucchini pulp into ¼-inch dice, and reserve it separately. Lightly salt the inside of the zucchini shells with the remaining ¼ teaspoon salt. Set them, hollow side down, on paper towels to drain while you prepare the filling.

3. Heat 1 tablespoon of the olive oil in a 12-inch skillet. Add the sausage and sauté until it is golden, using a spoon to break it into small pieces, about 6 minutes. Add the onions and cook until they are soft, 3 to 4 minutes. Add the chopped zucchini and cook for 2 minutes. Add the tomatoes and the remaining 1½ teaspoons garlic, and cook, stirring, until the moisture has evaporated and the filling comes together, 2 minutes. Remove the skillet from the heat, stir in the reserved 2 tablespoons breadcrumb mixture, and season with additional salt and pepper if necessary.

4. Preheat the oven to 350°F.

5. Rub the outside of the zucchini with the remaining ½ tablespoon olive oil, and season them lightly with salt and pepper. Turn the zucchini hollow side up, and lightly pat the insides with paper towels. Using a tablespoon or other small spoon, fill the zucchini with the warm filling. Top with the reserved breadcrumbs. Lay the zucchini in a baking dish, and bake for 30 minutes, or until golden brown and crispy on top.

6 to 8 servings

FRESH CROWDER PEAS

While these are simmering, they'll be comin' in the kitchen, asking, "What are you cooking?" and when you say, "Peas," they'll say, "Really...." The aroma from this pot ... ahhh yeah, baby. You won't disappoint with this one. In case you aren't yet familiar with crowder peas, which are so quintessentially Southern, they are very similar to fresh black-eyed peas. They differ in look (no distinctive black eye), and their ends are ever so slightly squared from being crowded in the pods.

2 tablespoons olive oil

½ cup diced green bell peppers (small dice)

½ cup diced onions (small dice)

½ cup diced carrots (small dice)

½ cup diced celery (small dice)

¼ teaspoon crushed red pepper

3 bay leaves

2 sprigs fresh thyme

2 teaspoons minced garlic

1 pound fresh crowder peas (frozen may be substituted if fresh are not available)

4 cups chicken stock or canned low-sodium chicken broth

1 tablespoon chopped fresh parsley leaves

¾ teaspoon salt

¼ teaspoon freshly ground black pepper

1. Heat the olive oil in a medium saucepan over medium-high heat. Add the green peppers, onions, carrots, celery, crushed red pepper, bay leaves, and thyme sprigs. Reduce the heat to medium and cook until the vegetables are tender, 5 minutes.

2. Add the garlic and cook, stirring, for 1 minute. Add the peas and stock, and bring to a boil. Reduce the heat to low and simmer for 25 to 30 minutes, or until the peas are tender.

3. Remove the thyme sprigs. Stir in the parsley, salt, and pepper, and serve warm.

About 1 quart, 2 to 4 servings

SPICED ZUCCHINI BREAD

Though we call this a bread, it's really more of a spice cake that uses grated fresh zucchini as a surprise ingredient. Serve it warm for breakfast, with cream cheese or butter and honey.

. . . .

3 eggs

¾ cup vegetable oil

1½ cups sugar

2 cups grated unpeeled zucchini

2 teaspoons vanilla extract

2½ cups all-purpose flour

1 tablespoon ground cinnamon

¾ teaspoon baking soda

¾ teaspoon salt

¼ teaspoon baking powder

¾ cup chopped lightly toasted walnuts or pecans

Cream cheese, at room temperature, for serving (optional)

1. Preheat the oven to 325°F, and grease two 8 × 4 × 2½-inch loaf pans.

2. In the bowl of an electric mixer, beat the eggs until foamy. Add the vegetable oil, sugar, zucchini, and vanilla extract and mix well. Add the flour, cinnamon, baking soda, salt, and baking powder, and mix until well blended. Stir in the nuts. Divide the batter evenly between the prepared loaf pans, and tap them gently on the counter to release any air bubbles.

3. Bake until the loaves have risen and are golden brown and a tester inserted into the center comes out clean, 55 to 60 minutes. Allow the bread to cool in the pans for 5 minutes; then turn the loaves out onto wire racks to cool.

4. Serve the bread warm, sliced and spread with cream cheese if desired.

2 loaves

Note: This bread is also great at room temperature or toasted, and it freezes well.

PUMPKIN CUSTARD PIE

Of course you can make a delectable pumpkin pie with fresh pumpkin. Where do you think the canned-pumpkin-puree people got the idea? Let's show 'em something. Use a ripe "sugar" or "pie" pumpkin to make the fresh puree, not the big, flavorless jack-o'-lantern type. Or visit your farmer's market and experiment with other varieties of pumpkins or other winter squash that they have to offer.

- -

1 recipe Pie Crust dough
   (recipe follows)

1 egg white, lightly beaten

2 cups Pumpkin Puree
   (recipe follows)

1¼ cups packed light brown sugar

½ cup packed dark brown sugar

4 eggs, lightly beaten

¾ cup heavy cream

1 tablespoon vanilla extract

¼ teaspoon ground cinnamon, plus
   extra for dusting

¼ teaspoon ground nutmeg

¼ teaspoon ground allspice

¼ teaspoon ground ginger

¼ teaspoon ground cardamom

Whipped cream, for serving

1. Place the pie crust dough on a lightly floured work surface, and roll it out to form a round that is about 13 inches in diameter and ⅛ inch thick. Working carefully, fit the round into a 10-inch deep-dish pie plate. Crimp the edges decoratively and then refrigerate the shell, lightly covered, for at least 1 hour and up to overnight.

2. Preheat the oven to 425°F.

3. Lightly coat one side of a piece of parchment paper with cooking spray, and position it, greased side down, on top of the chilled pie crust. Fill the crust with pie weights (dried rice or beans work fine) and blind-bake the crust until it is just set, 10 to 12 minutes. Remove the weights and parchment paper, and using a pastry brush, immediately brush the crust lightly with the egg white. Set it aside until cooled, about 20 minutes.

4. Reduce the oven temperature to 375°F.

5. Combine the pumpkin puree and all the remaining ingredients (except the whipped cream) in a large mixing bowl, and stir until well blended. Pour the filling into the pie crust, and bake until the custard is set and the crust is lightly golden, about 1 hour. (If the crust begins to brown too quickly, cover it with a rim of tented foil).

6. Let the pie cool completely. Slice, and serve with a dollop of whipped cream.

One 10-inch deep-dish pie, 8 to 10 servings

PIE CRUST

1¼ cups all-purpose flour

1 tablespoon sugar

¼ teaspoon salt

8 tablespoons (1 stick) cold unsalted butter, cut into pieces

3 to 4 tablespoons ice water

1. Place the flour, sugar, and salt in the bowl of a food processor, and pulse to combine. Add the butter and process until the mixture resembles coarse crumbs. While the machine is running, slowly drizzle in the water, 1 tablespoon at a time, and continue to process by pulsing until the dough just comes together to form a ball (you may not need to use all of the water, or you may need a bit more).

2. Transfer the dough to a lightly floured surface and shape it into a flat disk. Wrap it in plastic wrap and refrigerate it for at least 1 hour or up to overnight. (The dough can be frozen for up to a month; thaw it in the refrigerator before using.)

One 9- or 10-inch pie shell

PUMPKIN PUREE

One 5-pound sugar or "pie" pumpkin

Vegetable oil, for drizzling

1. Preheat the oven to 375°F. Line a baking sheet with parchment paper.

2. Cut the stem off the pumpkin and discard it. Cut the pumpkin in half; scoop out and discard the seeds. Cut the halves into quarters, and cut the quarters in half. Transfer the pumpkin pieces to the prepared baking sheet, and drizzle them with vegetable oil. Toss to coat well. Cover with aluminum foil, and bake until the pumpkin is tender (the tip of a knife should go in easily), 1 to 1½ hours.

3. Remove the baking sheet from the oven and set it aside until the pumpkin is cool enough to handle. Then peel the skin off (if it's not pulling off easily, use a paring knife), and chop the pulp into pieces. In batches, use a wooden spoon to push the pumpkin pieces through a sieve into a mixing bowl. Discard any fibrous parts that remain in the sieve.

4. Clean the sieve and line it with a coffee filter or cheesecloth. Transfer the pumpkin puree to the lined sieve and place the sieve over a bowl, making sure that the bottom of the sieve does not touch the bowl. Transfer this to the refrigerator and let it sit overnight to drain any excess liquid.

5. Discard the liquid and use the puree right away, or store it in an airtight container in the refrigerator for up to 1 week or freezer for up to 2 months.

About 2½ cups

nightshades

TOMATO TARTARE AND MICRO GREENS WITH SHALLOT VINAIGRETTE

I remember a time, not long ago, when the most widely available tomatoes were those developed to withstand the impact of long journeys across the country in less than perfect conditions and, hence, picked long before they were ripe. They looked good in the store but often lacked flavor. Nowadays, we can choose from Green Zebra, Cherokee Purple, Banana Legs, Golden Egg, Jersey Devil . . . and with names like those, how can you resist? This dish is best when the heirloom tomatoes are at their peak.

2 pounds heirloom tomatoes

1½ teaspoons salt

1 cup extra-virgin olive oil

6 to 8 sprigs fresh thyme

4 shallots, sliced into rounds (about ½ cup)

¼ cup brown rice vinegar

1 teaspoon minced garlic

1 teaspoon Dijon mustard

½ teaspoon sugar

2 tablespoons chopped fresh chives

1 tablespoon chopped fresh parsley leaves

1 tablespoon chopped fresh basil leaves

½ teaspoon freshly ground black pepper

2 cups cubed whole wheat bread (small cubes)

¼ cup chopped pitted black olives

½ cup micro greens

1. Seed and dice the tomatoes, and place them in a colander set over a bowl to catch the juices. Sprinkle ¾ teaspoon of the salt over the tomatoes, and let them sit while you prepare the rest of the dish.

2. Combine the olive oil, thyme, and shallots in a small saucepan. Bring to a boil, and then immediately reduce the heat. Simmer gently until the shallots are tender, 10 minutes. Remove the pan from the heat, and discard the thyme. Strain the shallots, reserving the oil separately, and allow them to cool. Puree the cooled shallots with 2 tablespoons of the reserved oil in a blender or food processor.

3. In a small bowl, whisk 3 tablespoons of the shallot puree with the vinegar, garlic, mustard, sugar, and herbs. Slowly whisk in 8 tablespoons of the reserved oil. Season with ½ teaspoon salt and ¼ teaspoon of the pepper. Set the vinaigrette aside.

4. Preheat the oven to 350°F.

5. In a medium mixing bowl, toss the bread cubes with ¼ teaspoon salt, the remaining ¼ teaspoon pepper, and 4 tablespoons of the remaining reserved oil.

Spread the bread cubes out on a baking sheet, and bake until crisp, 12 to 15 minutes. Set aside to cool.

6. In a large mixing bowl, combine the drained tomatoes, toasted bread cubes, and olives, and toss with ¼ cup of the shallot vinaigrette.

7. To assemble, place a 3-inch round cookie cutter on a plate, and spoon the tomato mixture into the mold, filling it all the way to the top. Remove the mold, and mound 2 tablespoons of the micro greens on top of the tomatoes. Drizzle the plate with a little of the remaining vinaigrette. Repeat this for all the remaining three plates, and serve.

4 servings

CHEESY CREOLE TOMATO PIE

Have too many ready-to-pick tomatoes in your garden? Try this pie, where the most delicious tomatoes are layered with cheese, sweet onions, breadcrumbs, and herbs. The quality of the tomatoes is crucial! If you are lucky enough to get Louisiana Creole tomatoes in the summertime, by all means use them for this recipe. Creole tomatoes have an unmistakable rich, deep tomato flavor that comes from the alluvial soil in which they are grown. Otherwise, any type of local vine-ripened tomato will do. And for the sweet onions you can use Texas 1015, Washington's Walla Walla, California's Imperial Sweet, or your own regional variety.

1 recipe Savory Pie Crust dough (recipe follows)

1 egg, separated

2 pounds ripe Creole tomatoes or other regional variety, such as heirlooms or beefsteak

½ teaspoon salt

¼ teaspoon freshly ground black pepper

4 tablespoons mayonnaise

⅓ cup unseasoned dry bread-crumbs

¾ cup thinly sliced Vidalia onions

1 tablespoon fresh thyme leaves

2 tablespoons thinly sliced fresh basil leaves

2 ounces Fontina cheese, grated (about ½ cup)

2 ounces mozzarella cheese, grated (about ½ cup)

2 tablespoons extra-virgin olive oil

2 tablespoons grated Parmigiano-Reggiano cheese

1. Roll out the pie dough on a lightly floured surface to fit a 9- or 10-inch deep-dish pie plate. Fit the dough into the pie plate and crimp the edges decoratively. Refrigerate, covered, for at least 30 minutes or up to a day.

2. Preheat the oven to 375°F.

3. Remove the pie shell from the refrigerator and line it with aluminum foil. Fill the shell with ceramic pie weights or dried beans, and bake for 13 minutes, or until lightly golden around the edges. Remove the foil and weights, return the shell to the oven, and bake for 3 minutes.

4. Remove the pie crust from the oven and place it on a wire rack. Lightly beat the egg white with a fork. Using a pastry brush, lightly coat the entire surface of the warm pie crust with the egg white (you will probably not use all the white). Then allow the pie shell to cool and the white to set. It will look glazed.

5. Slice the tomatoes into ¼-inch-thick rounds, discarding the stem and root ends. Season the tomatoes with the salt and pepper.

6. Combine the mayonnaise with the egg yolk in a small bowl, and stir until smooth.

7. Sprinkle one third of the breadcrumbs over the bottom of the cooled pie crust. Layer half of the sliced tomatoes over the breadcrumbs in a circular pattern, and top with half of the sliced onions. Drizzle in half of the mayonnaise mixture, and top with half of the herbs, half of the Fontina, half of the mozzarella, and half of the remaining breadcrumbs. Make a second layer with the remaining tomato slices, onions, mayonnaise mixture, herbs, Fontina, mozzarella, and breadcrumbs. Drizzle the olive oil over the top, and sprinkle with the Parmesan cheese.

8. Bake the pie in the oven for 50 minutes to 1 hour, until it is bubbly hot and golden brown. Allow it to cool for at least 30 minutes or up to 5 hours before serving. This pie is at its best at room temperature.

6 to 8 servings

SAVORY PIE CRUST

1¼ cups all-purpose flour

1 teaspoon salt

½ teaspoon freshly ground black pepper

8 tablespoons (1 stick) cold unsalted butter, cut into pieces

3 to 4 tablespoons ice water

1. Place the flour, salt, and pepper in the bowl of a food processor, and pulse to combine. Add the butter and process until the mixture resembles coarse crumbs. While the machine is running, gradually drizzle in the water, processing until the dough comes together to form a ball.

2. Transfer the dough to a lightly floured surface and shape it into a flat disk. Wrap it in plastic wrap and refrigerate it for at least 1 hour or up to overnight. (The dough can be frozen for up to a month; thaw in the refrigerator before using.)

One 9- or 10-inch pie shell

ROASTED TOMATO TAPENADE

I used heirloom Roma tomatoes for this recipe, but at the height of tomato season, when there are so many varieties to choose from, just about any variety of small, sweet tomato will work well here. Roasted tomatoes have a concentrated flavor, so remember, the better the tomato, the better the flavor. Use this tapenade as a spread for roasted vegetable sandwiches, tossed with pasta and olive oil for a quick pasta sauce, or on crostini for a quick hors d'oeuvre.

1½ pounds Roma (plum) tomatoes, cut in half lengthwise, seeds removed

3 tablespoons extra-virgin olive oil

1 teaspoon kosher salt

½ teaspoon freshly ground black pepper

3 sprigs fresh thyme

3 sprigs fresh rosemary

3 sprigs fresh marjoram

1 tablespoon minced garlic

1 teaspoon red wine vinegar

¼ cup finely chopped Kalamata olives (about 10 olives)

1. Preheat the oven to 450°F.

2. Combine the tomatoes, 2 tablespoons of the olive oil, and the salt and pepper in a medium mixing bowl.

3. Arrange the herb sprigs on a rimmed baking sheet or in a shallow baking dish. Dot the inside of each tomato half with some of the garlic. Lay the tomatoes, cut sides down, on top of the herbs and roast for 20 minutes, or until the skins are crackly. Remove the baking sheet from the oven and set it aside until the tomatoes are cool enough to handle.

4. Place the tomato halves and garlic on a cutting board. Add any juices, garlic, and herb leaves remaining in the pan to the cutting board (discard the whole herb sprigs). Finely chop the tomatoes and transfer them to a small bowl. Stir in the vinegar, olives, and remaining 1 tablespoon olive oil. Transfer the tapenade to a nonreactive container, cover, and refrigerate until ready to use. (The tapenade will keep for up to 1 week in the refrigerator.)

2 cups

WARM POTATO SALAD

I cannot resist the gorgeous baby potatoes that appear at the market. Grab a basket and fill it with all the different sizes, colors, and shapes—a pure expression of nature's bounty.

3 ounces (about 3 slices) applewood-smoked bacon, cut crosswise into ½-inch pieces

1 cup diced Texas 1015 or other sweet onions (small dice)

2 pounds baby potatoes, such as Ruby Crescent or fingerling

6 cups water

2 tablespoons plus ½ teaspoon salt

1 tablespoon whole-grain mustard

1 teaspoon freshly ground black pepper

1 tablespoon honey

¼ cup cider vinegar

½ cup grapeseed or other neutral vegetable oil

3 tablespoons minced fresh chives

1. Place the bacon in a small sauté pan and set it over medium-high heat. Cook until the bacon is crispy and the fat is rendered, about 5 minutes. Add the onions and cook until they are soft, about 4 minutes. Set aside.

2. Rinse and dry the baby potatoes. Cut them into ¼-inch-thick slices, and place them in a medium saucepan. Add the water and the 2 tablespoons salt, set the pot over high heat, and bring to a boil. Then reduce the heat and simmer until the potatoes are fork-tender, about 5 minutes. Drain the potatoes in a colander and set aside.

3. In a medium bowl, whisk together the mustard, pepper, honey, and vinegar. Add the oil in a steady stream while continuing to whisk. Add the chives and the remaining ½ teaspoon salt. Add the warm potatoes and the bacon-onion mixture, and stir gently to combine.

4. Transfer the potatoes to a shallow serving dish, and serve warm or at room temperature.

4 to 6 servings

EGGPLANT RELISH CROSTINI

This flavorful spread gets even better as it sits in the refrigerator—just make sure to return it to room temperature before serving. If you're an eggplant lover like I am, you could also toss this with cooked pasta for a quick meal.

¼ cup plus 2 tablespoons extra-virgin olive oil, plus more for drizzling

3 pounds eggplant (usually 2 large), peeled and cut into ½-inch cubes

1¼ teaspoons salt, plus more to taste

1 red bell pepper, roasted (see page 44) peeled, seeded, and minced (about ⅓ cup)

2 tablespoons chopped pitted Kalamata olives

1½ tablespoons chiffonade of fresh basil leaves (see Note)

1½ tablespoons red wine vinegar

2 teaspoons finely chopped drained nonpareil capers

2 teaspoons balsamic vinegar

1 teaspoon minced garlic

½ teaspoon crushed red pepper

French Bread Crostini (recipe follows), for serving

Finely grated Parmigiano-Reggiano or crumbled ricotta salata cheese, for garnish (optional)

1. Heat the 2 tablespoons olive oil in a large nonstick skillet over medium-high heat. When it is hot, add half of the cubed eggplant and sprinkle it with ½ teaspoon of the salt. Cook, stirring often, until the eggplant is tender and nicely caramelized, 8 to 10 minutes. Transfer the eggplant to a shallow bowl and set it aside. Repeat with another 2 tablespoons of the oil, the remaining eggplant, and another ½ teaspoon of the salt. Set the cooked eggplant aside until cooled to room temperature.

2. Once the eggplant has cooled, add all of the remaining ingredients (except the crostini and Parmesan), and stir gently to combine. Taste, and adjust the seasoning if necessary. Set the relish aside to allow the flavors to come together, at least 30 minutes and up to overnight. (Refrigerate if not using promptly but return to room temperature before serving.)

3. To serve, spoon the relish onto French Bread Crostini, drizzle with a little extra-virgin olive oil, and sprinkle with a little cheese if desired.

Note: "Chiffonade" is a French cooking term that refers to very thinly sliced strips or shreds of vegetables and/or herbs. This delicate cut is usually performed on lettuces or herb leaves, and is typically added at the end of cooking or used as a garnish.

3½ cups relish

FRENCH BREAD CROSTINI

One 12-inch French baguette or ficelle

6 to 8 tablespoons extra-virgin olive oil

½ teaspoon kosher salt

¼ teaspoon freshly ground black pepper

1. Preheat the oven to 325°F.

2. Cut the bread crosswise into ¼-inch-thick round or oval slices, and spread them out on a baking sheet. Brush the top of each slice with olive oil, and season them with the salt and pepper. Bake for 12 to 15 minutes, or until the crostini are light golden brown and crispy. Remove from the oven and let cool slightly before serving, or serve at room temperature.

20 to 24 crostinis

BAY, THYME, AND ROSEMARY ROASTED POTATOES

Here is a simple and scrumptious way to enjoy potatoes. You like baked potatoes, don't you? In this recipe, the potatoes roast on a bed of fresh herbs to highlight their intrinsically satisfying flavor.

2 pounds baby potatoes, such as Ruby Crescent or fingerling (no larger than 3 inches in diameter), rinsed and patted dry

¼ cup olive oil

1 tablespoon coarse sea salt

1 teaspoon hot smoked paprika

¼ teaspoon freshly ground black pepper

6 fresh bay leaves, or 3 medium dried

6 sprigs fresh thyme

3 sprigs fresh rosemary (each about 6 inches long)

2 tablespoons butter, at room temperature

1. Preheat the oven to 425°F.

2. Slice the potatoes in half lengthwise and place them in a medium bowl. Add the olive oil, salt, paprika, pepper, bay leaves, thyme sprigs, and rosemary sprigs. Toss thoroughly to combine. Arrange the herbs on a small rimmed baking sheet, and place the potatoes on top. Set the bowl aside.

3. Roast the potatoes for 20 minutes.

4. Remove the baking sheet from the oven and transfer the potatoes and herbs to the bowl you set aside. Toss well, and then carefully return the potatoes to the hot baking sheet. Roast for another 15 to 20 minutes, or until knife-tender.

5. Return the potatoes to the bowl one last time, and add the butter; toss the potatoes well, discard the bay leaves and herb sprigs, and serve immediately.

4 servings

EGGPLANT PARMESAN NAPOLEON WITH SPICY TOMATO SAUCE

There are as many varieties of eggplant as there are recipes for this highly versatile vegetable, but eggplant Parmesan is one of the most commonly known preparations and is a staple in my home repertoire. This recipe is a deconstructed version of that dish—it has a sophisticated presentation coupled with comforting, familiar flavors.

3 eggplants (about 1½ pounds each), sliced into ½-inch-thick rounds

2 teaspoons salt, plus more for sprinkling

2 tablespoons olive oil

2 tablespoons butter

1 cup diced onions (small dice)

4 large cloves garlic, minced

8 large vine-ripened tomatoes (6 to 8 ounces each), cored and cut into small dice

½ teaspoon freshly ground black pepper

¼ teaspoon cayenne pepper, or more to taste

2 teaspoons chopped fresh basil leaves, plus more for garnish

Peanut or canola oil, for frying

1 cup all-purpose flour

4 eggs, lightly beaten

2 cups dry unseasoned bread-crumbs

1½ pounds fresh mozzarella cheese, store-bought or homemade (see page 24), cut into ¼-inch-thick slices

1¼ to 2 cups finely grated Parmigiano-Reggiano cheese

1. Sprinkle both sides of the eggplant slices with salt, and set them aside on paper towels for about 30 minutes.

2. Meanwhile, prepare the sauce: Heat the olive oil and butter in a 2-quart saucepan over medium heat. When it is hot, add the onions and ¼ teaspoon of the salt and sauté, stirring frequently, until the onions are nicely browned and caramelized, about 6 minutes. Add the garlic and cook until fragrant, about 30 seconds. Add the tomatoes and simmer until they are tender and the sauce is slightly thickened, about 12 minutes. Add another ¼ teaspoon of the salt, the black pepper, the cayenne, and the chopped basil. Remove the sauce from the heat and set it aside to cool briefly. Then transfer the mixture to a blender, season it with ½ teaspoon of the salt, and puree (see Note). Set the sauce aside.

3. Quickly rinse the eggplant slices under cool running water, and then pat them dry with paper towels.

4. Position an oven rack about 6 inches from the broiler unit, and preheat the broiler.

5. Add enough oil to a large straight-sided sauté pan to reach ½ inch up the sides, and heat it over medium-high heat until it reaches a temperature of 375°F. Line one or two baking sheets with paper towels, and set them aside.

6. While the oil is heating, place the flour and beaten eggs in separate shallow pans that are large enough to hold the eggplant slices. Combine the breadcrumbs and the remaining 1 teaspoon salt in a third pan; whisk to blend.

7. Dip an eggplant slice in the flour, coating both sides and shaking off the excess. Dip the floured slice into the eggs, coating both sides. Then finally dredge the slice in the breadcrumbs, again coating both sides. Set the breaded eggplant aside on a tray. Repeat with the remaining eggplant slices.

8. In batches, place the breaded eggplant slices in the hot oil, taking care not to overcrowd the pan, and cook until they are golden brown and crisp, about 5 minutes per side. Transfer the eggplant to the prepared baking sheet to drain. Continue in this manner until all of the eggplant is cooked.

9. Place the eggplant slices on a clean baking sheet. Top each slice with 1 to 2 tablespoons of the tomato sauce and some of the sliced mozzarella, dividing the mozzarella among the eggplant slices. Sprinkle 1 tablespoon of the Parmesan over each. Transfer to the broiler and cook until the cheese is melted and bubbly, 1 to 2 minutes.

10. Carefully layer the eggplant slices on top of one another on six serving plates. Top with more tomato sauce, and garnish with chopped basil and any remaining Parmesan. Serve immediately.

6 servings

Note: Please use caution when blending hot liquids: blend only small amounts at a time, with the blender tightly covered and a kitchen towel held over the top.

SAUSAGE-STUFFED BELL PEPPERS

Calling all you pepper lovers out there—you know who you are! Check out this simple riff on the classic rice and meat–stuffed pepper. Sweet, mild Italian sausage is the key here, and the fresh tomato in the stuffing adds so much moisture that you don't even need a sauce!

. . . .

5 large green bell peppers, sliced in half lengthwise, seeds removed

3 tablespoons extra-virgin olive oil

12 ounces fresh sweet Italian sausage, removed from casings and crumbled

1½ cups chopped onions

2 tablespoons minced garlic

1¼ cups chopped ripe tomatoes

3 tablespoons minced fresh basil leaves

½ teaspoon salt, plus more if needed

1 teaspoon freshly ground black pepper, plus more if needed

2 cups cooked long-grain rice

3 tablespoons fine dry unseasoned breadcrumbs

6 tablespoons freshly grated Parmigiano-Reggiano cheese

1. Bring a large pot of heavily salted water to a boil. Add 8 of the pepper halves to the boiling water, in batches if necessary, and cook for 2 minutes. Transfer the peppers to a colander and run them under cool water briefly to stop the cooking. Then transfer the pepper halves to a large plate or a baking sheet lined with paper towels, and set aside to cool.

2. Preheat the oven to 375°F.

3. Chop the remaining pepper halves and set them aside.

4. Add 1 tablespoon of the olive oil to a medium skillet, and add the sausage. Cook over medium-high heat, breaking the sausage into small pieces with a spoon, until it is browned, 4 to 6 minutes. Add the onions, chopped bell pepper, and garlic, and cook, stirring often, until the vegetables are very soft and caramelized, about 6 minutes. Add the tomatoes and cook until they have softened and the liquids have been released, about 2 minutes. Add the basil, salt, and pepper and mix well. Stir in the rice and remove from the heat. Taste, and adjust the seasoning if necessary.

5. Spoon the sausage-rice mixture into the bell pepper halves. Combine the breadcrumbs and cheese in a small bowl, and sprinkle the mixture evenly over the stuffed peppers. Place the peppers in a baking dish, and pour about ½ inch of water into the dish. Drizzle the tops of the peppers with the remaining 2 tablespoons olive oil. Bake until the tops are crusty and brown, and the peppers are heated through, 30 to 35 minutes.

4 servings (2 peppers each)

POBLANO AND HATCH CHILE STEW

Hatch chiles have become famous nationwide, prized for their unique flavor. Grown in the fertile Hatch/Mesilla Valley in New Mexico, these green chiles have a robust and earthy taste with varying amounts of heat. They are harvested in September and are celebrated at the Hatch Valley Chile Festival in New Mexico, where the chiles can be sampled in all forms from roasted to raw. They are available throughout the Southwest through early October. If you are unable to acquire Hatch chiles for this recipe, try one of their close relatives, the Anaheim.

6 poblano chiles

4 Hatch chiles

3 tablespoons canola oil

1 cup chopped red bell peppers

1 cup chopped onions

1 clove garlic, minced

3 quarts cold water, chicken stock, or canned low-sodium chicken broth

2 cups cubed peeled Idaho potatoes (1-inch cubes)

2 teaspoons kosher salt

1 bay leaf

¼ cup chopped fresh cilantro leaves

Sour cream, crème fraîche (see page 134), or tortilla chips, for serving (optional)

1. Roast the poblano and Hatch chiles according to the instructions on page 44.

2. Coarsely chop the peppers. You should have about 2 cups chopped roasted poblano chiles and 1 cup chopped roasted Hatch chiles. Set them aside.

3. Heat the oil in a large saucepan over medium-high heat, and when it is hot, add the bell peppers, onions, and garlic. Sauté until the onions are golden brown, about 4 minutes. Add the water, potatoes, salt, and bay leaf, and bring to a boil. Then reduce the heat to a simmer and cook until the potatoes are tender, about 45 minutes.

4. Add the chopped roasted chiles and cook for another 20 minutes.

5. Stir in the cilantro. Ladle the stew into individual serving bowls and serve immediately, topped with sour cream, crème fraîche, or tortilla chips, if desired.

Warning: Please use plastic gloves when handling hot chiles, or make sure to wash your hands well after handling.

8 servings

TOMATO, ZUCCHINI, AND LEEK GALETTE WITH ROASTED GARLIC GOAT CHEESE

This is no ordinary pie. The vegetables roast beautifully on top of golden puff pastry, and in between there is a scrumptious goat cheese spread (which is also delicious served with your favorite toast, so make extra!). We like to use beautiful heirloom tomatoes, but any of the best medium-size ripe local tomatoes will do.

1 sheet frozen puff pastry, thawed

3 tablespoons olive oil

2 cups thinly sliced well-washed leeks (white part only)

Salt and freshly ground white pepper

1 pound medium heirloom tomatoes, stem ends trimmed

8 ounces zucchini, ends trimmed

5 tablespoons extra-virgin olive oil

5 ounces goat cheese, at room temperature

1 teaspoon fresh thyme leaves

2 heads Roasted Garlic (see method on page 171)

½ cup finely grated Parmigiano-Reggiano cheese

2 tablespoons thinly sliced fresh basil leaves

1. On a lightly floured surface, roll out the puff pastry dough to 1/16-inch thickness. Cut out a 12-inch round, and place it on a rimmed baking sheet lined with parchment paper. Chill the dough in the freezer for at least 15 minutes or up to an hour.

2. Preheat the oven to 450°F.

3. Heat the olive oil in a 10-inch sauté pan over medium to medium-low heat. Add the leeks, ½ teaspoon salt, and ⅛ teaspoon white pepper. Cook, stirring as needed, until the leeks have softened, 5 to 7 minutes. Remove the pan from the heat and transfer the leeks to a plate; let them cool until you're ready to assemble the galette.

4. Slice the tomatoes into ¼-inch-thick rounds, and arrange them in one even layer on a wire rack set over a baking sheet. Sprinkle with ¼ teaspoon salt, and set aside to drain for 10 minutes.

5. Meanwhile, slice the zucchini into ⅛-inch-thick rounds. In a small bowl, mix the zucchini slices with 1 tablespoon of the extra-virgin olive oil, ¼ teaspoon salt, and ⅛ teaspoon white pepper. Set aside.

6. In a medium-size bowl, combine the goat cheese, thyme, ½ teaspoon salt, ¼ teaspoon white pepper,

and 2 tablespoons of the extra-virgin olive oil. Mix well with a rubber spatula. Squeeze each head of roasted garlic over the bowl, pressing the soft cloves out of the peel. Mix until the goat cheese is smooth and the mixture is uniform.

7. Remove the baking sheet from the freezer (it is okay if the dough is frozen—it will soften by the time you complete the assembly) and spread the goat cheese mixture evenly over the dough, leaving a 1-inch border around the edges. Spread the sautéed leeks evenly over the goat cheese. Blot the tomatoes dry and arrange them in a concentric pattern over the leeks. Arrange the zucchini slices in a concentric pattern over the tomatoes. Sprinkle the Parmesan evenly over the top. Fold the border of the pastry up and over the edge of the tomatoes.

8. Bake the galette for 20 minutes, or until the crust is golden and puffed.

9. Remove the galette from the oven, sprinkle the fresh basil over the top, and drizzle with the remaining 2 tablespoons extra-virgin olive oil. Set the galette aside for at least 15 minutes before slicing and serving.

4 servings

ROASTED TOMATILLO SALSA

Tomatillos, which are sometimes called husk tomatoes, originated in Mexico and Guatemala and are a standard component in traditional cooking there. The popularity of the tomatillo in the United States paralleled the influx of Mexicans and Guatemalans. Tomatillos are a green fruit encased in a paper-thin husk that must be removed before cooking. They are generally the size of a small tomato, or even as small as a cherry tomato, and their flesh is white and meaty. Tomatillos have a lemony flavor with sweet and sour notes. They can be used raw in soups and salsas or roasted to bring out their unique flavor.

1 pound tomatillos, husked and rinsed

6 cloves garlic, unpeeled

1 small onion, quartered

1½ tablespoons olive oil

Salt and freshly ground black pepper

1 jalapeño, stemmed, seeded, and minced

Juice of 1 lemon

Juice of 1 lime

1. Preheat the oven to 400°F.

2. Place the tomatillos, garlic, and onion quarters on a baking sheet. Drizzle with the olive oil and season with salt and pepper to taste. Roast the vegetables in the oven until they are browned and softened, 15 to 20 minutes.

3. Place the tomatillos and onion in the bowl of a food processor. Squeeze the garlic cloves out of their peels into the food processor. Add the jalapeño, lemon juice, and lime juice, and pulse until the mixture is thoroughly combined but still slightly chunky. Season the salsa with salt and pepper to taste. Set it aside to cool to room temperature before serving.

4. Serve with crisp tortilla chips or in any way in which you would use salsa. Tomatillo salsa will keep for up to 1 week, refrigerated in a covered, nonreactive container.

2½ cups

berries, figs, and melons

RASPBERRY BELLINI WITH HOMEMADE RASPBERRY SYRUP

Fresh raspberries are always such a treat—but their delicate nature means that they do not have a long shelf life. One way to preserve them is by making a simple raspberry syrup. Here we combine the syrup with sparkling wine for a beautiful, refreshing cocktail.

1 tablespoon Raspberry Syrup (recipe follows)

3 ounces Prosecco or other dry sparkling wine

Fresh raspberries, blackberries, or sliced peaches, for garnish

Place the raspberry syrup in the bottom of a champagne flute. Fill the glass with the Prosecco, garnish with the fresh fruit, and serve.

1 serving

RASPBERRY SYRUP

This syrup is also excellent drizzled over ice cream, pancakes, or waffles, or stirred into club soda for homemade raspberry soda.

1 cup sugar

¼ cup Chambord liqueur

¼ cup water

2 pints fresh raspberries

1. Combine the sugar, Chambord, and water in a small saucepan and bring to a boil, stirring occasionally to dissolve the sugar. Add the raspberries and cook for 10 to 12 minutes, until softened and beginning to break down.

2. Strain the mixture into a bowl through a fine-mesh sieve lined with cheesecloth. Discard the solids. Transfer the syrup to a glass jar, cover, and refrigerate for up to 4 weeks. (Or store the syrup in a plastic container in the freezer for up to 6 months.)

2 cups

WATERMELON LIMEADE

Wow! This flavor-packed limeade is a real thirst quencher during the dog days of summer, when watermelon is at its best. Should a festive occasion arise, it also makes a wonderful margarita mixer when paired with premium white tequila.

8 cups cubed watermelon (seeds removed), or 1 quart watermelon juice

1 cup freshly squeezed lime juice

½ cup sugar, or more to taste

Lime slices, for garnish (optional)

1. Place half of the watermelon cubes in a blender and process until smooth. Strain through a fine-mesh sieve set over a large bowl; discard the solids. Repeat with the remaining watermelon cubes. You should end up with about 1 quart of watermelon juice.

2. Add the lime juice and sugar to the watermelon juice, and stir until the sugar has dissolved. Taste, and add more sugar if necessary. Transfer the limeade to a nonreactive pitcher and refrigerate until thoroughly chilled.

3. Serve over ice in tumblers, with lime slices for garnish.

5 cups, 4 to 6 servings

LEMON-SCENTED BLUEBERRY PANCAKES

These simple pancakes are a great way to give fresh blueberries the starring role. Since the pancake batter is not very sweet, these are best enjoyed with maple syrup. If you're not a syrup lover, I would suggest adding a bit more sugar to the batter.

1 cup fresh blueberries, picked over for stems

1 cup all-purpose flour

1 tablespoon corn flour or finely ground cornmeal

2 tablespoons sugar

¾ teaspoon baking powder

½ teaspoon salt

¼ teaspoon baking soda

¾ cup buttermilk

6 tablespoons whole milk

4 tablespoons (½ stick) unsalted butter, melted, plus more butter for cooking and serving

1 egg, lightly whisked

½ teaspoon finely grated lemon zest

½ teaspoon vanilla extract

Maple syrup, for serving

1. Combine the blueberries and 2 teaspoons of the flour in a small bowl, and toss to coat well. Set aside.

2. Place the remaining flour and the corn flour, sugar, baking powder, salt, and baking soda in a medium mixing bowl, and whisk to combine.

3. Combine the buttermilk and milk in a separate mixing bowl. In a small bowl, whisk the melted butter and egg until well combined; then stir the egg mixture into the buttermilk mixture. Add the lemon zest and vanilla, and stir well. Add the wet ingredients to the dry ingredients, and stir until just combined; do not overmix. Gently fold the blueberries into the batter, and set it aside to rest while the skillet is heating.

4. Place a nonstick skillet over medium heat. When a drop of water dances across the surface, it is ready. Add a small pat of butter to the skillet, and then add about ⅓ cup batter for each pancake, fitting in as many as you can while leaving enough room to turn the pancakes. Cook until they are bubbly around the edges and the top surface is beginning to look slightly dry, 2 to 3 minutes. Turn them over and continue to cook until the pancakes are golden on the bottom and just cooked through, 1 to 2 minutes. Place on a warm plate and cover lightly with aluminum foil while you cook the remaining pancakes.

5. Serve the pancakes hot, with butter and maple syrup.

About 10 pancakes, 4 servings

WATERMELON, FETA, AND ARUGULA SALAD WITH WATERMELON VINAIGRETTE

Watermelon and feta may seem to be an unlikely combination, but I assure you it is fantastic. The sweetness of the watermelon balances perfectly with salty feta cheese; add a little peppery arugula from the garden, and this salad is sure to be a hit at your next dinner party.

½ small jalapeño, stem and seeds removed

3 tablespoons red currant jelly

4 cups diced watermelon (seeds removed, ½-inch dice)

¼ cup white wine vinegar

¼ teaspoon minced garlic

¼ teaspoon salt

⅛ teaspoon freshly ground black pepper

1 tablespoon olive oil

6 cups baby arugula, rinsed and spun dry

½ cup sliced red onions

⅓ cup crumbled feta cheese, or to taste

Freshly cracked black pepper, for garnish

1. Combine the jalapeño, red currant jelly, 1 cup of the diced watermelon, the vinegar, garlic, salt, and pepper in the bowl of a food processor, and process until smooth. With the machine still running, drizzle in the olive oil. Store the vinaigrette in the refrigerator until ready to use, up to 2 days. Shake well before using.

2. In a large bowl, toss the arugula with a bit of the dressing. Mound the greens in the center of a large flat serving dish, and surround them with the remaining diced watermelon and the onions. Scatter the feta over the salad. Garnish with cracked black pepper to taste. Serve with the remainder of the dressing on the side.

4 to 6 servings

CANTALOUPE AND PANCETTA CREAM SAUCE FOR PASTA

I know, I know. This sounds crazy, right? Well, you just have to trust me on this one. The cantaloupe breaks down to form the backbone of a sweet, creamy sauce scented with pancetta and marjoram. A sleeper but a keeper, for sure.

3 tablespoons unsalted butter

2 ounces sliced pancetta, diced

¼ cup minced shallot

3 cups diced ripe cantaloupe
(from 1 medium cantaloupe)

½ cup heavy cream

½ teaspoon salt

¼ teaspoon freshly ground black
pepper, plus more for garnish

1 teaspoon minced fresh marjoram
leaves

8 ounces spaghetti rigati, linguine,
or fettucine

½ cup freshly grated Parmigiano-
Reggiano cheese

1. Bring a large pot of salted water to a boil.

2. Heat 1 tablespoon of the butter in a large sauté pan or Dutch oven over medium-high heat. Add the pancetta and cook, stirring frequently, until it is crisp and has rendered most of its fat, 3 to 4 minutes. Add the shallot and cook, stirring, until softened, 1 to 2 minutes. Add the remaining 2 tablespoons butter, and when it has melted, add the melon. Cook, stirring frequently, until the melon completely breaks down and forms a smooth, thick sauce, 8 to 10 minutes.

3. Add the heavy cream, salt, pepper, and marjoram, and cook until the cream has reduced by half and the sauce has a smooth, thick consistency that coats the back of a spoon, about 3 minutes. Remove the sauce from the heat.

4. Add the pasta to the boiling water, stir well, and cook until al dente (about 10 minutes). Drain well, reserving ½ cup of the pasta cooking water.

5. Add the hot pasta and ¼ cup of the Parmesan to the warm sauce. Return the pan to medium heat, and toss until the pasta is nicely coated with sauce and heated through. Should the sauce seem too thick, add a bit of the pasta cooking water to help toss the pasta and thin the sauce.

6. Serve the pasta immediately, garnished with the remaining Parmesan cheese and with freshly ground black pepper.

4 appetizer servings

RICOTTA NAPOLEONS WITH FRESH BERRIES

Slightly sweetened soft ricotta cheese and fresh-picked berries sandwiched between crispy phyllo cookies: a truly delightful summer dessert. Both the ricotta filling and the phyllo cookies can be made several days in advance. If fresh berries are out of season, use sliced ripe stone fruits or fresh figs instead.

1 pound fresh ricotta cheese (see page 23)

3 tablespoons superfine sugar

2 tablespoons freshly squeezed lemon juice

1 tablespoon vanilla extract

⅛ teaspoon ground nutmeg

8 sheets phyllo dough

8 tablespoons (1 stick) unsalted butter, melted

½ cup granulated sugar

½ pint fresh strawberries, hulled and halved

½ pint fresh blackberries

Confectioners' sugar, for garnish

1. Place a medium colander or strainer inside a large bowl, making sure that the bottom of the colander does not touch the bottom of the bowl. Line the inside of the colander with a piece of cheesecloth, folded in half. Place the ricotta inside the cheesecloth, and cover with plastic wrap. Refrigerate for 24 hours to let the excess liquid drain off the ricotta.

2. Remove the cheesecloth and ricotta from the colander, discard the plastic wrap, and gently squeeze the cheesecloth to extract any excess liquid. Place the ricotta in a medium bowl, and stir in the superfine sugar, lemon juice, vanilla, and nutmeg. Refrigerate, covered, until ready to use.

3. Preheat the oven to 375°F.

4. Place the phyllo on a sheet of waxed paper, and cover it with a towel to keep it from drying out; replace the towel each time you remove a sheet of phyllo. Brush a large baking sheet with some of the melted butter. Place a piece of phyllo on the buttered baking sheet, and lightly brush the top with butter. Sprinkle a fine layer of sugar over the butter. Repeat this process with all the phyllo, sugar, and butter. Carefully cut the dough into 3-inch squares, and bake until the phyllo turns golden brown, about 20 minutes. Remove the phyllo from the oven and set it aside to cool.

5. To make the napoleons, place one of the phyllo squares on a plate. Spoon ¼ cup of the ricotta mixture onto the phyllo, arrange one fourth of both berries on top of the ricotta mixture, and top with a second phyllo square. Repeat with the remaining phyllo squares, ricotta, and berries. Dust with confectioners' sugar, and serve immediately.

4 servings

SPICED BLACKBERRY SOUP WITH CARAMELIZED PEACHES AND CANDIED ALMONDS

Peaches and blackberries are perfect partners, as they come into season just about the same time each summer. The slightly tart flavor of the berries nicely balances the sweetness of the peaches. This recipe calls for goat's milk yogurt, but if this is not available, or if you simply prefer it, cow's milk yogurt is a fine substitute.

4 cups fresh blackberries

1 cup peach juice

½ cup honey

¼ cup water

1 tablespoon freshly squeezed lime juice

¼ teaspoon ground cinnamon

⅛ teaspoon ground nutmeg

¼ teaspoon vanilla extract

12 ounces goat's milk yogurt

Caramelized Peaches (page 117)

Candied Almonds (recipe follows)

1. In a large, heavy saucepan, combine the blackberries, peach juice, honey, water, lime juice, ground cinnamon, and nutmeg. Bring to a boil. Then reduce the heat to a low simmer and cook for 20 minutes, or until the berries have softened.

2. Remove the pan from the heat and let the mixture cool slightly. Then strain the berry mixture through a fine-mesh sieve into a small bowl, pressing to extract as much liquid as possible; discard the solids. Add the vanilla and 8 ounces (1 cup) of the yogurt to the strained blackberry mixture, and whisk until well blended. Refrigerate covered until thoroughly chilled, at least 2 hours and up to overnight.

3. Serve the soup in chilled bowls, garnished with slices of Caramelized Peaches, a dollop of the remaining yogurt, and a few pieces of the Candied Almonds.

1 quart, 4 to 6 servings

CANDIED ALMONDS

Use these to garnish desserts or salads.

1 egg white, whipped to soft peaks

¼ cup sugar

⅛ teaspoon ground cardamom

1 cup slivered almonds, toasted

⅛ teaspoon rose water (optional),
see Note

1. Preheat the oven to 375°F. Line a baking sheet with parchment paper.

2. In a small bowl, combine the egg white, sugar, cardamom, and toasted slivered almonds. Toss well to combine. Sprinkle the almonds with the rose water, if using, and spread them out on the prepared baking sheet. Roast in the oven for 12 minutes, stirring once midway through to ensure even browning. Remove from the oven and set aside to cool.

3. When the almonds are cool enough to handle, either chop them or break them into smaller pieces. They can be stored in an airtight container at room temperature for up to 1 month.

1 cup

Note: Rose water is simply an essence obtained from the distillation of rose petals. It is said to have originated in the Middle East and is used primarily as a flavoring for food. Rose water is a common flavoring in Iranian, Indian, and Turkish cuisine, especially for sweets. It can be found in international markets or in the international aisle of your grocery store.

CARAMELIZED PEACHES

Luckily for us, peaches have a fairly long season—usually from the end of May through September. The best peaches are those that have been left on the tree until the very last minute, allowing the sugars to fully develop. Peaches should be slightly firm to the touch, with a light floral scent. For this recipe, use peaches that are firm-ripe so that they do not fall apart as you cook them. These caramelized peaches are so versatile, they can be used in sweet and savory dishes alike. They are wonderful with the dandelion greens salad on page 45, and spooned over vanilla ice cream.

4 firm-ripe peaches

1 cup ruby port

½ cup sugar

4 whole cardamom pods

1 cinnamon stick (3 inches long)

1 whole vanilla bean, split
  lengthwise

1. Cut the peaches in half, remove the stones, and slice each half into quarters.

2. In a medium saucepan over medium-high heat, combine the port, sugar, cardamom pods, cinnamon stick, and vanilla bean, and bring to a boil. Reduce the heat to medium and cook until the mixture is somewhat syrupy, about 3 minutes. Add the peaches, stir to coat, and cook until they are golden and are nicely coated in the syrup, 3 to 4 minutes. Discard the whole spices, and serve the peaches warm or cool.

2 cups

RUSTIC BLACKBERRY COBBLER

This old-fashioned American classic just screams "Fourth of July" to me!

4 pints fresh blackberries, rinsed briefly and drained

¾ cup sugar

2 tablespoons cornstarch

2 teaspoons freshly squeezed lemon juice

1½ cups all-purpose flour, plus more for dusting and rolling out

2 teaspoons baking powder

¼ teaspoon salt

6 tablespoons cold unsalted butter, cut into pieces

¾ cup plus 2 tablespoons heavy cream

½ teaspoon vanilla extract

Vanilla ice cream or whipped cream, for serving (optional)

1. Preheat the oven to 375°F.

2. In a large mixing bowl, combine the berries with ½ cup of the sugar, the cornstarch, and the lemon juice. Toss well. Place the berry mixture in a deep-dish pie plate and cover it with foil. Set the pie plate on a baking sheet (to catch any juices that may bubble over later), and transfer it to the oven. Bake until the berries begin to release their juices and soften, 15 to 20 minutes.

3. While the berries are baking, combine 3 tablespoons of the remaining sugar with the flour, baking powder, and salt in a mixing bowl. Add 4 tablespoons of the butter and work it in with a pastry blender, two forks, or your fingers until the mixture resembles coarse crumbs. Add the ¾ cup heavy cream and the vanilla, and stir until the mixture just comes together to form a dough. Turn the dough out onto a lightly floured surface and dust it lightly with flour. Using a lightly floured rolling pin, roll the dough to a thickness of about ½ inch. Using a 2½-inch floured cutter, cut the dough into 8 rounds.

4. When the berries have softened, remove the baking dish from the oven and remove the foil covering. Stir the berries well to distribute the juices. Arrange the dough rounds on top of the berries. Brush the rounds with the remaining 2 tablespoons heavy cream, and sprinkle the remaining 1 tablespoon sugar over them. Scatter the remaining butter pieces over the hot berries. Return the baking dish to the oven and cook until the biscuits are golden brown and the berries are hot and bubbly, 25 to 30 minutes.

5. Remove the dish from the oven and allow the cobbler to cool for 15 to 20 minutes before serving. Serve warm, spooned into shallow bowls and garnished with vanilla ice cream or whipped cream if desired.

6 to 8 servings

BLACK MISSION FIGS STUFFED WITH BLUE CHEESE AND LAVENDER HONEY

Fresh figs are the ultimate local fruit. They don't travel well. They come from either your local farm, a grocery that carries local produce, or your neighbor's tree. If you're fortunate enough to get your hands on a few pints, embellish them as below. Though we suggest Black Mission figs here, you can certainly use any variety that's available.

4 tablespoons honey

2 tablespoons dried lavender flowers, plus more for garnish

2 ounces creamy blue cheese such as Valdeon, Gorgonzola dolce, or any Rogue Creamery blue cheese

½ cup mascarpone cheese

12 fresh firm-ripe Black Mission figs, stem ends trimmed

1. Combine the honey and the 2 tablespoons lavender flowers in a small saucepan, and warm over low heat. Remove from the heat and steep the lavender in the honey for at least 10 minutes. Strain the honey into a small bowl and discard the solids.

2. In a small bowl, combine the blue cheese with the mascarpone and half of the lavender honey. Stir until almost smooth (it is okay if it is slightly chunky).

Place the blue cheese mixture in a pastry bag fitted with a plain tip (or in a plastic bag with one corner snipped), and set it aside until ready to serve. (Refrigerate the bag briefly if the mixture becomes too soft.)

3. Using a paring knife, cut downward lengthwise into each fig, as if you were preparing to cut the fig in half, but cut only about halfway through the fig. Turn the fig 90 degrees and make a second cut perpendicular to the first in the same manner. Using your fingers, gently pry open the top portions of the fig to create space for the cheese mixture. Pipe the blue cheese mixture into the figs. Arrange the figs on a serving plate, and garnish them with lavender flowers. Drizzle the figs with the remaining lavender honey, and serve at room temperature.

6 servings

the orchard

PINK LADY APPLE MARTINI

This is a wonderful fall cocktail made with Pink Lady apples. You can serve it as outlined below, or instead of adding the sugar to the blender, coat the rims of the glasses with the sugar (run a wedge of lemon around the rims first to help it stick). If you have sparkling sanding sugar for the rims, even better.

2 Pink Lady apples, cut into ½-inch chunks

1 cup vodka

4 teaspoons apple juice

1 tablespoon superfine sugar

1 teaspoon freshly squeezed lemon juice

1 cup ice cubes

1. Chill four to six martini glasses in the freezer for at least 10 minutes.

2. Combine the apples, vodka, apple juice, sugar, and lemon juice in a blender, and blend for 30 seconds on high speed, or until smooth. Strain the mixture through a fine-mesh sieve (or a cheesecloth-lined strainer) into a bowl, firmly pressing the solids with a flexible spatula or the back of a spoon to extract as much liquid as possible. Chill the liquid in the refrigerator until ready to serve.

3. Place the ice in a cocktail shaker. Add the apple mixture and shake vigorously until well chilled. Strain into the chilled serving glasses, and serve immediately.

4 to 6 servings

SPINACH, CHERRY, AND GOAT CHEESE SALAD WITH WARM BACON DRESSING

Fresh sweet cherries make this salad special—it's definitely a wonderful way to enjoy them when they are in season, which is typically from late spring to early summer. If you happen to live in cherry country—mostly the cooler climates of Northern California, Washington, Oregon, and New York—consider yourself lucky. Try to find beautiful plump, deep reddish-black cherries for this recipe.

8 ounces sliced bacon, diced

½ cup finely chopped red onion

1 teaspoon minced garlic

¼ teaspoon freshly ground black pepper, plus more if needed

Pinch of salt, plus more if needed

1½ tablespoons Creole or other coarse-grain mustard

¼ cup red wine vinegar

2 tablespoons sugar

¼ cup vegetable oil

8 cups fresh spinach, tough stems removed, leaves washed and spun dry (about 12 ounces)

1 cup fresh cherries, pitted and cut in half

4 ounces goat cheese, crumbled

1. Cook the bacon in a large skillet over medium-high heat until crisp, about 5 minutes. Using a slotted spoon, transfer the bacon to a plate lined with paper towels to drain. Pour off all but ¼ cup of the rendered bacon drippings from the skillet.

2. Add the onion to the drippings remaining in the skillet, and cook, stirring, over medium-high heat until soft, about 3 minutes. Add the garlic, pepper, and salt and cook, stirring, for 30 seconds. Add the mustard and vinegar and cook, stirring, to deglaze the pan. Add the sugar and stir to dissolve it. Remove the skillet from the heat and whisk in the oil. Return the bacon to the skillet and adjust the seasoning to taste.

3. Divide the spinach evenly among six salad plates. Arrange the cherries around the edges, scatter the goat cheese over the top, and drizzle the warm bacon dressing over the salad. Serve immediately.

6 servings

APPLE TARRAGON GRANITA

Once this begins to freeze, you will be astounded at the color: shiny ice crystals with bright green flecks. The flavor is delicately herby and amazingly refreshing. This *is* the granita of all granitas! Serve this as dessert or as a palate cleanser between courses.

½ cup sugar

½ cup fresh tarragon leaves (from about 4 large sprigs)

3 cups apple juice

4 teaspoons freshly squeezed lemon juice

1. Place the sugar and tarragon in a food processor or blender, and pulse until the tarragon is finely ground and the sugar is green. Transfer the tarragon sugar to a medium bowl; add the apple juice and lemon juice, and whisk to combine. Let the mixture stand for 10 minutes, stirring it occasionally, until the sugar has dissolved.

2. Pour the mixture into a 9-inch square nonreactive metal baking pan, and place it in the freezer. Stir the mixture, pulling a fork back and forth through it every 45 minutes or so for 4 hours, or until frozen. The mixture will become a fluffy, icy concoction.

3. To serve the granita, spoon it into chilled dishes.

4 to 6 servings

APRICOT CLAFOUTI

This is a French country dessert that is traditionally made with cherries, but the tart-sweet flavor of in-season apricots makes for a nice alternative. The texture falls somewhere between a custardy cake and a pancake, and the clafouti is delicious served warm from the oven. The almond flour adds a little bit of nutty sweetness.

3 tablespoons butter

½ cup all-purpose flour, plus more for dusting the baking dish

3 eggs

¾ cup whole milk

¾ cup heavy cream

1 tablespoon brandy

1 whole vanilla bean

¾ cup almond flour

½ cup sugar

½ teaspoon salt

1¼ pounds (about 6) apricots, halved and pitted

Confectioners' sugar, for garnish (optional)

¼ cup sliced almonds, lightly toasted, for garnish (optional)

1. Preheat the oven to 350°F. Butter an oval 1½-quart gratin dish, about 12 by 8½ inches or other dish of similar size, with 1 tablespoon of the butter, and then dust it with a bit of flour to coat the bottom and sides of the dish; tap the dish to expel any extra flour.

2. Melt the remaining 2 tablespoons butter. In a medium mixing bowl, combine the eggs, milk, heavy cream, brandy, and melted butter. Using a small knife, slice the vanilla bean down the middle and scrape out the tiny seeds. Discard the bean (or save it for another purpose), and add the seeds to the egg mixture.

3. In a separate medium mixing bowl, combine the almond flour, all-purpose flour, sugar, and salt, and stir to blend. Add the dry ingredients to the wet ingredients, and whisk until just incorporated.

4. Spread the apricots across the bottom of the prepared baking dish, cut sides down. Pour the batter over the apricots. Bake until the clafouti is golden brown and just firm, with a spongelike texture, about 45 minutes. Remove from the oven and let it cool for 10 minutes before serving.

5. Garnish, if desired, with confectioners' sugar and toasted almonds.

6 to 8 servings

BRAISED APPLES, ROASTED ACORN SQUASH, AND FRESH THYME

Don't worry about cutting the squash and apples into perfect cubes—just make them uniform in size. Once these babies come together in the end, it will be a tender, buttery, sweet, tart, herby mix—all that nature has to offer. It is shown with the Pan-Roasted Duck Breasts with Apple Cider Reduction on page 266.

. . . .

2¾ pounds acorn squash, peeled (see Note), halved, seeded, and cut into roughly ½-inch dice (about 4 cups)

3 tablespoons butter, melted

½ teaspoon ground cinnamon

¼ teaspoon ground nutmeg

½ teaspoon salt

2 tablespoons butter

⅓ cup diced red onion (small dice)

¼ teaspoon freshly ground white pepper

2 Fuji or Gala apples, cut into roughly ½-inch dice (about 2 cups)

½ cup chicken stock or canned low-sodium chicken broth

1 teaspoon chopped fresh thyme leaves

1. Preheat the oven to 450°F. Line a small baking sheet with parchment paper.

2. In a medium bowl, toss the squash with the melted butter, cinnamon, nutmeg, and ¼ teaspoon of the salt. Transfer the squash to the prepared baking sheet, and roast in the oven for 15 minutes, or until golden and fork-tender. Remove from the oven and set aside to cool for at least 5 minutes.

3. Heat the 2 tablespoons butter in a small saucepan over medium-high heat. Add the onion, the remaining ¼ teaspoon salt, and the pepper and cook until the onion is soft, about 2 minutes. Add the diced apples and the chicken stock, and bring to a simmer. Cook for 5 minutes, or until the apples are barely tender. (Don't cook the apples too long—you want them to retain their shape.) Remove from the heat.

4. In a medium mixing bowl, combine the roasted squash, the thyme, and the braised apples with their cooking liquid. Toss gently to combine, and serve warm.

4 servings

Note: To peel acorn squash: Peeling acorn squash is similar to peeling a pineapple. Use a serrated knife (bread knife) and slice off each end. With the squash resting on one end, and holding it steady with one hand, use the tip of the knife to cut from top to bottom, following the curve of the squash. To cut around the ridge you will have to cut a bit deeper into the squash; just follow the curve as closely as you can. Continue until you have peeled the entire squash.

NECTARINE AND MASCARPONE TART IN A SUGAR COOKIE CRUST

The nectarines and mascarpone here are a play on the quintessential flavor combo of peaches and cream, and they work extremely well together. The result is a simpler and lighter version of cheesecake that will impress even the most hard-core cheesecake aficionados. The uncooked nectarines give this tart a cool, fresh quality.

25 sugar cookies, coarsely broken (about 6 ounces; about 2¼ cups pieces)

4 tablespoons (½ stick) unsalted butter, melted

One 8-ounce container mascarpone cheese

8 ounces cream cheese, at room temperature

¼ cup sour cream

½ cup sugar

¼ teaspoon vanilla extract

⅛ teaspoon almond extract

4 or 5 small firm-ripe nectarines, halved, pitted, and thinly sliced

¼ cup peach jam, warmed

1. Preheat the oven to 350°F.

2. Finely grind the sugar cookies in a food processor. Add the melted butter, and blend until the crumbs are evenly moistened. Press the mixture over the bottom and up the sides of a 9-inch tart pan with a removable bottom. Bake until the color darkens, pressing the sides with the back of a spoon if they begin to slide, about 8 minutes. Remove from the oven, set aside on a wire rack, and allow to cool completely.

3. Combine the mascarpone, cream cheese, sour cream, sugar, vanilla extract, and almond extract in a medium bowl, and beat with a handheld electric mixer on low speed until smooth. Spread this filling in the cooled crust. Cover loosely, and refrigerate until the filling is set, for at least 2 hours and up to 1 day.

4. Carefully arrange the nectarine slices on top of the chilled filling, fanning the slices out in concentric circles to cover as much of the tart as possible. Brush with the warm jam.

5. Serve immediately, or cover and refrigerate for up to 6 hours before serving.

8 servings

PEAR TARTLETS WITH HOMEMADE CRÈME FRAÎCHE

A beautiful, impressive dessert for a holiday table that looks like much more trouble than it is. Make the filling and cut out the pastry rounds the day before you want to serve these, and they will come together in no time.

. . . .

1 large egg

⅓ cup plus 3 teaspoons sugar

3½ tablespoons all-purpose flour

4 tablespoons (½ stick) unsalted butter

1 vanilla bean, split lengthwise

1 tablespoon finely grated orange zest

¼ teaspoon ground cardamom

2 pinches freshly ground black pepper

8 ounces frozen puff pastry, thawed but still cold

3 firm-ripe pears, such as Anjou

1 lemon, halved

¼ cup apricot preserves

Homemade Crème Fraîche (recipe follows) or vanilla ice cream, for serving

1. In a small bowl, whisk the egg with the ⅓ cup sugar until blended. Add the flour and stir to combine.

2. Combine the butter, vanilla bean, orange zest, cardamom, and pepper in a small, heavy saucepan, and cook over high heat until the butter is light golden brown and has a nutty aroma, about 3 minutes. Remove the vanilla bean, scraping the seeds into the melted butter. (Discard the scraped vanilla bean pod or reserve it for another use.) Allow the butter to cool slightly; then add it to the flour mixture and stir well to combine. Allow to cool to room temperature. Then refrigerate, covered, until thoroughly chilled, about 1 hour. (This filling can be prepared up to 3 days in advance.)

3. Cut the puff pastry sheet in half, and roll each half out to approximately ⅛-inch thickness. Using a sharp knife and a small plate as a guide, cut out three 6-inch rounds from each piece of puff pastry. Transfer the rounds to two ungreased baking sheets, cover with plastic wrap, and refrigerate for 30 minutes or up to overnight.

4. Preheat the oven to 375°F.

5. Using a sharp knife, cut approximately 1 inch off the top of each pear, so that the remaining fruit is more or less spherical. Peel, halve, and core the pears.

Rub them with the juice of half a lemon to keep them from discoloring. Place 1 pear half, cut side down, on a work surface, and slice it crosswise into about ⅛-inch-thick slices. Do not separate the slices. Repeat with the remaining pear halves. Squeeze more lemon juice over the sliced pears. Reserve any uneven pieces and the end pieces separately.

6. Remove the puff pastry rounds from the refrigerator, and place 1 heaping tablespoon of the butter filling in the center of each round. Using 1 pear half for each round, decoratively fan the slices in a tight, overlapping circle so that they cover the pastry round. The slices should not extend beyond the edge of the pastry. (If you like, cut any uneven slices or end pieces of pear into small wedge-shaped pieces and place them in the center of the tartlets to form rosettes.) Sprinkle ½ teaspoon of the remaining sugar over each tartlet, and bake for about 30 minutes, or until the pears are tender and the tartlets are lightly browned around the edges.

7. While the tartlets are baking, heat the apricot preserves in a small saucepan (thin them with a small amount of water if necessary).

8. Use a pastry brush to gently brush the top of each tartlet with some of the warm preserves. Serve warm or at room temperature, with a dollop of Homemade Crème Fraîche or vanilla ice cream, as desired.

6 servings

HOMEMADE CRÈME FRAÎCHE

A recipe for do-it-yourself thickened cream with a subtle nutty flavor.

1 teaspoon well-shaken buttermilk

1 cup heavy cream

1. Combine the buttermilk and cream in a small saucepan, and heat gently to lukewarm (100°F). Transfer the mixture to a small container and let it sit, lightly covered, at room temperature until thickened to the consistency of sour cream. Depending on the temperature of the room, this can take between 12 and 36 hours, with overnight being the general rule.

2. Stir the thickened crème fraîche. Cover, and refrigerate until ready to use. It will continue to thicken and take on a tangier flavor as it ages. The crème fraîche will keep for up to 10 days.

1 cup

cole crops:
broccoli, cabbage, and cauliflower

ROASTED BRUSSELS SPROUTS

This is a simple dish but, oh, so good. The Brussels sprouts end up sweet and tender, with crispy edges and a light coating of lemony, garlicky, Parmesan goodness.

2 pounds Brussels sprouts, stem ends trimmed, halved lengthwise

5 tablespoons olive oil

1 teaspoon salt

½ teaspoon freshly ground black pepper

1 teaspoon minced garlic

½ teaspoon grated lemon zest

¼ cup finely grated Parmigiano-Reggiano cheese, plus more to taste

1. Preheat the oven to 375°F.

2. Toss the Brussels sprouts in 3 tablespoons of the olive oil, and season with the salt and pepper. Transfer them to a baking sheet and spread them out in one even layer.

3. Roast until the Brussels sprouts are crisp-tender and lightly caramelized around the edges, 20 to 25 minutes. Immediately transfer them to a large mixing bowl, and add the remaining 2 tablespoons olive oil, minced garlic, lemon zest, and Parmesan. Toss to coat evenly, sprinkle with more Parmesan as desired, and serve.

4 servings

BRAISED KOHLRABI WITH FENNEL AND LEEKS

Kohlrabi has been described as an ideal garden vegetable as long as you don't plant too much. It is a very productive plant and is easy to grow. Though it is the child of "wild cabbage" and literally means "cabbage turnip," it has been neglected in our repertoire. Maybe this is because its flavor is less assertive than its other family members—broccoli, cauliflower, and asparagus. We don't know why, because it's good! Try it.

2 tablespoons olive oil

1 tablespoon butter

3 large heads kohlrabi, cut into
½-inch-thick wedges

2 leeks, white and light green
parts, well rinsed in several
changes of water and sliced
into ¼-inch-thick rounds

1 large bulb fennel, cored and sliced

¼ cup dry white wine

3 cups vegetable or chicken stock,
or canned low-sodium vegetable
or chicken broth

4 sprigs fresh thyme

3 sprigs fresh fennel fronds, plus
1 tablespoon chopped

1 teaspoon salt

½ teaspoon freshly ground white
pepper

1. Combine the olive oil and butter in a large, deep sauté pan. Once the butter has melted and the foam has subsided, add the kohlrabi, leeks, and fennel. Cook for 4 to 5 minutes, browning the kohlrabi on both sides. Add the wine and cook until it has reduced by half. Then add the vegetable stock, thyme, and fennel fronds, and season with the salt and pepper. Cook, partially covered, for 20 minutes, or until the vegetables are crisp-tender.

2. Remove the thyme sprigs. Serve the vegetables in a shallow bowl with some of the braising liquid, garnished with the chopped fennel fronds.

4 servings

EMERIL'S QUICK CABBAGE IN BEER

This salty-sweet caramelized cabbage is the perfect accompaniment to the Honey-Brined Pork Chops with Nectarine Chutney on page 268.

4 tablespoons (½ stick) butter

2 cups chopped onions

3 bay leaves

½ teaspoon crushed red pepper

1 tablespoon minced garlic

1 teaspoon salt

One 4- to 5-pound cabbage, cored and chopped into 2-inch pieces

One 12-ounce bottle American lager–style beer

1. Melt the butter in a 12-inch or larger skillet over medium-high heat. Add the onions, bay leaves, crushed red pepper, garlic, and salt, and cook for 3 minutes. Raise the heat to high and add half of the cabbage. Cook, stirring as needed, until the cabbage begins to caramelize and shrinks in the pan, about 6 minutes. Add the remaining cabbage and cook for another 6 minutes, stirring as needed and scraping up any caramelized bits.

2. Add the beer, reduce the heat to low, and cook until the cabbage is flavorful and tender, 5 to 6 minutes. Serve hot.

6 to 8 servings

CURRY-SCENTED ROASTED CAULIFLOWER

Oh, babe. Don't let the simplicity of this recipe fool you. This quick dish is da bomb and would be right at home on your dinner table next to roasted chicken or grilled meats. Dig in!

2 small heads cauliflower (3 to 3½ pounds total), cored and cut into medium florets

6 tablespoons ghee or clarified butter, melted (see Notes)

2 teaspoons kosher salt

2 teaspoons curry powder

½ teaspoon cayenne pepper

¼ teaspoon garam masala (see Notes)

1. Preheat the oven to 400°F.

2. Place the cauliflower in a large mixing bowl.

3. In a smaller mixing bowl, combine the ghee and all the remaining ingredients. Stir to blend well, and then pour the spice mixture over the cauliflower. Toss until the cauliflower is thoroughly coated with the ghee and spices.

4. Transfer the cauliflower to a large baking sheet, and roast until it is caramelized around the edges and crisp-tender, 18 to 20 minutes, stirring it once midway through cooking. Serve hot.

Notes: Ghee is butter that has been slowly melted until the solids and liquid separate. The solids fall to the bottom and the butter is cooked until the milk solids are browned and the moisture evaporates, resulting in a nutty, caramel-like flavor. This last step is what defines ghee from regular clarified butter. Ghee is used primarily in Indian cooking, but is wonderful for any high-heat cooking preparation since it has a higher smoke point than butter. You can find it in many Middle Eastern markets or you can easily make your own at home.

Garam masala is a blend of ground Indian spices that comes in many variations, but can include black pepper, cinnamon, cloves, coriander, cumin, cardamom, dried chiles, fennel, mace, nutmeg, and other spices. Garam means "warm" or "hot" in Indian. Today it is easy to find commercially bottled garam masala in the spice aisle of most grocery stores.

4 to 6 servings

TUSCAN KALE AND WHITE BEAN RAGOUT

Tuscan kale—also known as Lacinato kale, black kale, and dinosaur kale—is one of my favorite greens. Its dark green, puckered leaves are hearty and hold up well in any dish. Braise it with onions, garlic, bay leaf, and white beans . . . talk about a meal-in-one!

2 tablespoons olive oil

1 bay leaf

2 cloves garlic, smashed and roughly chopped

¼ teaspoon crushed red pepper

1 small red onion, sliced

1½ pounds Tuscan kale, rinsed, patted dry, and cut crosswise into 1-inch-wide slices

¾ teaspoon kosher salt, plus more if needed

¼ teaspoon freshly ground black pepper, plus more if needed

3½ cups cooked white beans, or two 15-ounce cans cannellini beans or white beans, drained and rinsed

1 cup canned diced tomatoes, with their juices

½ cup vegetable or chicken stock, or canned low-sodium vegetable or chicken broth

Extra-virgin olive oil, for drizzling

1. Heat the olive oil in a large sauté pan over medium-high heat. When it is hot, add the bay leaf, garlic, crushed red pepper, and red onion. Cook until the onion begins to wilt and the garlic begins to turn golden around the edges, 3 to 4 minutes. Add the kale, salt, and pepper, and cook for another 2 minutes. Then add the white beans, tomatoes, and stock. Cover, and cook until the kale is wilted and cooked through, about 15 minutes. Taste, and adjust the seasoning if necessary.

2. Transfer the ragout to a serving dish, and drizzle it with extra-virgin olive oil to taste. Serve hot.

4 to 6 servings

BRAISED BROCCOLI RABE

The assertive flavor of broccoli rabe gets a boost here from the fragrant toasted garlic and crushed red pepper . . . just the way they do it in parts of Italy. This simple side dish would be wonderful alongside the Braised Lamb Shanks on page 275 and the Creamy Polenta on page 219.

¼ cup olive oil

¾ teaspoon crushed red pepper

3 tablespoons thinly sliced garlic

2 bunches broccoli rabe, cut ends trimmed (about 2 pounds total)

1½ cups chicken stock or canned low-sodium chicken broth

1 teaspoon salt

1. Heat the olive oil in a large skillet over medium heat. When it is hot but not smoking, add the crushed red pepper and garlic, and cook until fragrant, 30 to 45 seconds. Add the broccoli rabe in batches, stirring between additions, and cook until slightly wilted, about 2 minutes. Add the stock and salt, stir to combine, and cover the skillet. Cook until the greens are just tender, stirring occasionally, 4 to 5 minutes.

2. Transfer the broccoli rabe to a serving bowl, and continue to cook the braising liquid until it has reduced by half, about 2 minutes. Drizzle the braising liquid over the broccoli rabe, and serve hot.

4 servings

thistles, stalks, and pods

FRIED OKRA WITH CREAMY BUTTERMILK DIP

Ahhhh, the abundance of okra. In the South, it's available fresh practically all year-round. Fry up these bites, whip up the dip, and make some friends.

Vegetable oil, for deep-frying

1 cup buttermilk

1 egg

2 tablespoons Louisiana hot sauce, or your favorite

1 cup all-purpose flour

1 cup yellow cornmeal

2 teaspoons cayenne pepper

2 teaspoons granulated garlic

1 tablespoon salt, plus more for seasoning

1 teaspoon freshly ground black pepper

2 pounds okra, sliced into ½-inch-thick rounds (about 4 cups)

Creamy Buttermilk Dip (recipe follows)

1. Heat the oil in a deep-fryer to 360°F. (See Note below.)

2. In a small bowl, whisk the buttermilk, egg, and hot sauce to combine. In a second bowl, combine the flour, cornmeal, cayenne, granulated garlic, the 1 tablespoon salt, and the black pepper.

3. Working in batches, dredge the okra first in the buttermilk mixture, allowing any excess to drip off, then in the flour mixture. Shake to remove any extra breading. Repeat until all of the okra is breaded.

4. Fry the okra, in batches, in the hot oil, turning it as necessary, until lightly golden, about 5 minutes. Transfer the fried okra to paper towels to drain, and season lightly with salt. Repeat with the remaining okra.

5. Serve the okra hot, with the Creamy Buttermilk Dip on the side for dipping.

Note: If you don't own a deep-fryer, see step 5 on page 50 for instructions on frying in a Dutch oven. Make sure to keep the temperature of the oil as close to 360°F as possible.

About 4 servings

CREAMY BUTTERMILK DIP

¾ cup buttermilk

½ cup mayonnaise, store-bought or homemade (see page 153)

¼ cup sour cream

½ teaspoon cayenne pepper

1 teaspoon minced garlic

1 tablespoon chopped fresh chives

Salt, to taste

Combine the buttermilk, mayonnaise, sour cream, cayenne, garlic, and chives in a small bowl, and stir to mix well. Add salt to taste. Serve immediately, or cover and refrigerate until ready to serve (up to 1 day in advance).

About 1½ cups

Buttermilk
#25-31
OPEN
PUSH UP
HERE
1L
1000 mL
3/4
750
1/2
500
1/4
250

ARTICHOKES ALLA ROMANA

This classic Italian artichoke preparation leaves you with only the tender heart and the softest leaves, so you can eat the whole thing with a fork and knife. Don't be afraid to pare the artichoke way down—this is an important step in ensuring that only the tender parts remain.

2 lemons, halved

4 large globe artichokes

3 tablespoons extra-virgin olive oil

2 cloves garlic, sliced

2 tablespoons nonpareil capers, drained

1 cup dry white wine

1 cup water

1 teaspoon salt

1 tablespoon chopped fresh parsley leaves

1 tablespoon chopped fresh oregano leaves

½ teaspoon crushed red pepper

1. Fill a large bowl with cold water. Add the juice of 1 lemon, and set it aside.

2. One artichoke at a time, remove three or four rows of the outer leaves, until the exposed leaves are light green, and then slice off about two-thirds of the top of the artichoke. The furry choke should be exposed. Using a small spoon, scoop into the heart of the artichoke to remove the prickly choke and the fine hairs that cover the top of the artichoke heart. While you are paring them, rub the artichokes frequently with a lemon half to prevent browning.

3. Trim off the very end of each artichoke stem, leaving as much of the stem as possible, and then use a paring knife to peel the stem, removing the tough outer layer. Cut the artichokes in half lengthwise, and if necessary, remove any bits of choke that remain. Place the artichokes in the bowl of lemon water to prevent them from oxidizing.

4. Heat the olive oil in a large sauté pan, and then add the artichokes, sliced garlic, and capers. Cook over medium heat for 2 minutes. Add the white wine, water, the juice of half a lemon, and the salt. Cover the pan and cook the artichokes for 30 minutes, or until almost all of the liquid has reduced.

5. Add the chopped parsley, oregano, and the crushed red pepper, and cook for another 5 minutes. The artichokes should be tender at this point. Check by inserting a sharp paring knife into the heart: it should not meet any resistance.

6. Serve the artichokes with the remaining pan juices.

4 servings

GARDEN CELERY WITH HOMEMADE PIMENTO CHEESE

This retro combination never fails to please. The homemade mayo and freshly roasted red bell peppers really boost this pimento cheese into a league all its own.

8 ounces sharp cheddar cheese, grated, at room temperature (about 2 cups)

½ cup Emeril's Homemade Mayonnaise (recipe follows)

⅓ cup minced roasted red bell pepper (about 1 red bell pepper, roasted, peeled, seeded, and minced; see page 44)

2 teaspoons grated red onion

¼ teaspoon plus ⅛ teaspoon kosher salt, or to taste

¼ teaspoon Louisiana hot sauce

⅛ teaspoon cayenne pepper

6 celery stalks, ends trimmed and any fibrous strings removed, cut into thin batons for dipping, chilled

1. Combine all the ingredients except the celery in a medium bowl, and stir to blend well. Refrigerate until slightly chilled. (The pimento cheese can be refrigerated for up to 2 days; allow it to warm up slightly before serving.)

2. Serve the pimento cheese in small bowls, garnished with the celery batons for dipping.

About 1½ cups pimento cheese, 6 appetizer servings

EMERIL'S HOMEMADE MAYONNAISE

1 large egg, at room temperature

1 large egg yolk, at room
temperature

1½ teaspoons freshly squeezed
lemon juice, or more to taste

½ teaspoon Dijon mustard

½ teaspoon minced garlic

½ teaspoon kosher salt, or more to
taste

¼ teaspoon ground white pepper
or cayenne pepper, or more to
taste

1 cup vegetable oil

¼ cup olive oil

1. In the bowl of a food processor fitted with the metal blade, combine the egg, egg yolk, lemon juice, mustard, garlic, salt, and pepper. Process on high speed until smooth, light yellow, and frothy, about 1 minute. While the processor is still running, combine the vegetable and olive oils in a measuring cup with a pour spout, and working very slowly, add the oil to the processor in a thin, steady stream, processing until the oil is completely incorporated and a thick emulsion is formed. (It is very important that the oil is added very slowly, especially at the beginning; otherwise the mayonnaise may break.)

2. Transfer the mayonnaise to a nonreactive bowl, and add more salt, pepper, and/or lemon juice if desired. Use immediately, or refrigerate in a nonreactive airtight container for up to 1 day.

1½ cups

GRASS-FED BEEF CARPACCIO WITH SHAVED CELERY IN A WHITE WINE VINAIGRETTE, DRIZZLED WITH LEMON-INFUSED OIL

The celery adds a nice crunchy texture to this dish and is highlighted by the tangy vinaigrette and lemon-infused oil. We call for grass-fed beef because it's like Mother Nature intended. Feeding cows native grasses and allowing them to graze at the grass's nutritional peak only brings good things for the cow, for us, and for the environment.

10 ounces grass-fed beef tenderloin

½ cup extra-virgin olive oil

Zest of 1 lemon, removed with a vegetable peeler

3 tablespoons dry white wine, such as Sauvignon Blanc

1 tablespoon white wine vinegar

1 tablespoon minced shallot

¼ teaspoon minced garlic

½ teaspoon honey

½ teaspoon Dijon mustard

½ teaspoon salt

¼ teaspoon freshly ground white pepper

½ cup plus 1 tablespoon olive oil

1 teaspoon finely chopped fresh parsley leaves

1 teaspoon finely chopped fresh chives

1 teaspoon kosher salt, plus more for seasoning

½ teaspoon cracked black pepper, plus more for seasoning

¾ cup very thinly sliced celery (half-moons)

½ cup fresh celery leaves

Shaved Parmigiano-Reggiano cheese, for garnish

1. Wrap the tenderloin well in plastic wrap, and then place it inside a resealable sandwich bag, squeezing out any excess air and sealing the bag. Freeze the meat for at least 2 hours, or until mostly frozen.

2. While the beef is freezing, make the lemon-infused olive oil: Place the extra-virgin olive oil and the lemon zest in a small saucepan. Bring to a gentle simmer and cook for about 5 minutes. Cover the pan, remove it from the heat, and allow it to stand, undisturbed, for about 30 minutes. Then strain the oil through a fine-mesh sieve and reserve it. (Discard the zest.)

3. To make the vinaigrette, place the white wine, vinegar, shallot, garlic, honey, mustard, ¼ teaspoon of the salt, and ⅛ teaspoon of the white pepper in a blender and blend well. With the blender running, add the remaining ½ cup olive oil in a slow, steady stream, processing until the vinaigrette is emulsified. Transfer the vinaigrette to a small mixing bowl, and stir in the parsley and chives. Set it aside until ready to use.

4. Remove the tenderloin from the freezer and season it on all sides with the kosher salt and cracked black pepper. Heat the 1 tablespoon olive oil in a medium-size sauté pan over high heat. When it is hot, add the tenderloin and sear until nicely browned and caramelized on all sides, about 1 minute per side. Remove from the pan and refrigerate until cool, 15 to 20 minutes.

5. Remove the cooled tenderloin from the refrigerator and cut it against the grain into ⅛-inch-thick slices. Place several slices on a sheet of plastic wrap (making sure there is sufficient space between the slices) and lay another sheet of plastic wrap on top. Using a mallet, pound the slices until they are paper-thin, being careful not to tear any of the slices. Repeat until all of the slices are flattened. Arrange the slices, slightly overlapping, in a circle on each of four serving dishes, and season them lightly with kosher salt and cracked black pepper.

6. Place the sliced celery and celery leaves in a small mixing bowl. Add the remaining ¼ teaspoon salt and ⅛ teaspoon white pepper. Drizzle with about 1 tablespoon of the vinaigrette, and toss to coat well. Mound the celery in the center of the carpaccio, dividing it evenly among the four plates. Drizzle with the vinaigrette and the lemon-infused oil. Garnish with the Parmesan shavings, and serve.

4 servings

NEW ORLEANS–STYLE STUFFED ARTICHOKES

The Italian-American community in New Orleans just loves stuffing beautiful globe artichokes with an intensely seasoned breadcrumb mixture and then braising them until they are fork-tender. Now, be forewarned: these do take a bit of time to prepare, and if stuffed properly, they end up *big*! But they are worth the time, and just one easily satisfies a manly appetite. Do like my friends in the test kitchen do and drizzle them with some of the lemony braising liquid before serving.

5 cups fine dry unseasoned breadcrumbs, preferably homemade (see Note)

1½ cups finely grated Parmigiano-Reggiano cheese

½ cup finely grated Pecorino Romano cheese

⅓ cup minced fresh parsley leaves

⅓ cup minced fresh basil leaves

¼ cup finely chopped green onions (green tops only)

2 tablespoons minced fresh oregano leaves

1 teaspoon minced fresh thyme leaves

1 teaspoon crushed red pepper (or less, to taste)

1 teaspoon freshly ground black pepper

½ teaspoon cayenne pepper

½ cup plus 2 tablespoons extra-virgin olive oil

½ cup hot water

1 tablespoon freshly squeezed lemon juice

1 teaspoon grated lemon zest

½ cup olive oil

3 tablespoons minced garlic

2 tablespoons minced anchovies (about 8 canned anchovy fillets)

1 teaspoon salt

2 lemons, halved

4 large (10-ounce) globe artichokes

1. In a large bowl, combine the breadcrumbs, Parmesan, Pecorino, parsley, basil, green onions, oregano, thyme, crushed red pepper, black pepper, and cayenne, and stir well to blend. In a separate bowl, combine ¼ cup of the extra-virgin olive oil with the hot water, lemon juice, and lemon zest, and whisk to blend. Drizzle the olive oil mixture over the breadcrumbs, and stir until the crumbs are evenly coated. Set aside.

2. Heat the olive oil in a medium skillet over medium heat. When it is hot, add the garlic and anchovies and cook until fragrant, 1 to 2 minutes. Pour the hot oil-garlic mixture over the breadcrumb mixture, and stir to blend. Set the stuffing aside.

3. Fill a large nonreactive Dutch oven with 1 inch of water. Add the 2 tablespoons extra-virgin olive oil, the salt, and a lemon half, cut into pieces. Heat over medium-low heat while you prepare the artichokes. (If the water comes to a boil before the artichokes are stuffed, cover the pot and keep warm.)

4. Slice off the upper third of each artichoke, and rub the cut portions with a lemon half. Trim the stems to about ½ inch, so that the artichokes will sit upright. Using scissors, trim the thorns from the ends of the remaining leaves; remove any damaged leaves with a paring knife. Using a spoon or a melon baller, scoop out the choke and the hairy portion of each artichoke, leaving a cavity in the center for stuffing. Rub or squeeze the lemon half over all the cut portions of each artichoke.

5. One at a time, stuff the artichokes: Beginning with the outer leaves and progressing towards the middle, stuff the leaves with the breadcrumb mixture, pressing lightly to compact the stuffing. When you reach a place where the leaves are too tight to pry apart, fill the center cavity with stuffing. Repeat with the remaining artichokes. Cut one of the remaining lemon halves into thin slices, and top each artichoke with a lemon slice. Squeeze the remaining lemon half over the artichokes, and drizzle 1 tablespoon of the extra-virgin olive oil over each artichoke.

6. Place the artichokes in the Dutch oven—ideally they should fit tightly in the pot so as to hold each other upright during cooking. Cover the pot and bring the liquid to a boil. Reduce the heat to a low simmer and cook, covered, testing the artichokes occasionally, until the leaves are very tender and pull away easily, 1¼ to 1½ hours.

7. Remove the artichokes from the pot and allow them to cool for at least 15 minutes before serving. Serve hot or warm, drizzled with some of the cooking juices if desired.

Note: Homemade breadcrumbs can be made fresh or dry. Fresh breadcrumbs are made by placing pieces of fresh, soft bread into a food processor until the desired size of crumb is reached. Dry breadcrumbs are often made from day-old French bread that has been cubed and either left to dry or toasted in a low oven until dry. The cubes are then cooled and processed in a food processor until the desired size of crumb is reached. Any sort of seasoning or flavoring can be added to either fresh or dry breadcrumbs—many folks drizzle with olive oil and add chopped fresh herbs or finely grated cheese. Homemade fresh and dry breadcrumbs should not be used interchangeably, but both can add a nice texture to a dish.

4 servings

RHUBARB STRAWBERRY CRISP

Rhubarb and strawberries are a classic duo that appears in farmer's markets and grocery stores at the same time each year, letting us know that spring has officially arrived. Look for rhubarb stalks that are deep red and firm to the touch, and deep red strawberries that are firm, fragrant, and not bruised.

1 pound rhubarb, trimmed and diced

1 pound strawberries, halved or quartered if large

¾ cup granulated sugar

2 tablespoons cornstarch

2 teaspoons freshly squeezed lemon juice

⅔ cup all-purpose flour

⅔ cup rolled oats

¾ cup packed light brown sugar

6 tablespoons (¾ stick) cold unsalted butter, cut into small pieces

1 teaspoon ground cinnamon

½ teaspoon freshly grated nutmeg

¼ teaspoon salt

Vanilla ice cream, for serving (optional)

1. Preheat the oven to 375°F. Lightly butter a deep-dish pie plate or other shallow 1½- to 2-quart nonreactive baking dish, and set it aside.

2. Combine the rhubarb, strawberries, sugar, cornstarch, and lemon juice in a medium mixing bowl and toss to combine. Transfer the mixture to the prepared baking dish, and set it aside while you prepare the topping.

3. Combine all the remaining ingredients in the bowl of an electric mixer fitted with the paddle attachment, and process on low speed until the mixture is crumbly and coarse.

4. Sprinkle the topping over the fruit, and then place the baking dish on a rimmed baking sheet (to catch any juices that may bubble over). Transfer it to the oven and bake until the topping is golden brown and crisp, and the juices are bubbly and glossy, 40 to 45 minutes. Set aside to cool briefly, then serve hot or warm, with a scoop of vanilla ice cream if desired.

6 to 8 servings

roots, shoots, tubers, and bulbs

BRAISED LEEKS WITH A MUSTARD VINAIGRETTE

This is a wonderful way to enjoy fresh leeks when they are in season. The leeks become sweeter as they are cooked, but they still retain a nice oniony flavor. The tangy, herbaceous Dijon vinaigrette would taste good on many things, but it really complements the leeks here. Bon appétit!

6 large leeks (about 7½ inches long and 2 inches wide)

4 cups chicken stock or canned low-sodium chicken broth

¼ cup dry white wine

¼ cup extra-virgin olive oil

Juice of 1 lemon

2¾ teaspoons salt

1 teaspoon black peppercorns

1 bay leaf

4 or 5 sprigs fresh thyme

¼ cup red wine vinegar

1 tablespoon minced shallot

2 teaspoons Dijon mustard

¼ teaspoon freshly ground black pepper

½ cup vegetable oil

¼ cup olive oil

1 tablespoon chopped fresh parsley leaves

1 tablespoon chopped fresh chives

1. Trim off enough of the root ends of the leeks to dispose of the roots yet still keep the leek halves held together. Trim the tops so that only the white and some of the light green portion remains. (Discard the dark green tops or reserve them for another use.) Clean the leeks thoroughly by holding them under cold running water. (If your leeks are very dirty and it's hard to clean them without cutting the root ends off completely, do as we did in the photo: Simply trim the root ends. This will allow you to separate the leaves and run them under cool running water to rinse them thoroughly of any sand or grit. Then tie the halves back together with kitchen twine. This will keep the halves together when you braise them.)

2. Place the leeks in a large, deep sauté pan, and add the chicken stock, white wine, extra-virgin olive oil, lemon juice, 2 teaspoons of the salt, the peppercorns, bay leaf, and thyme sprigs. Bring to a gentle boil, weighting the leeks down with a small heatproof plate or other heatproof object in order to keep them submerged. There should be enough liquid to cover the leeks; if not, add a bit of water. Reduce the heat to a simmer and cook until the leeks are very tender when pierced with the tip of a knife, 12 to 15 minutes.

3. While the leeks are poaching, make the vinaigrette: In a small mixing bowl, combine the vinegar, shallot, mustard, black pepper, and the remaining ¾ teaspoon salt, and whisk to combine. Let stand for 5 to 10 minutes. Then combine the vegetable oil and olive oil in a measuring cup, and while whisking constantly, slowly drizzle the oil into the vinegar-shallot mixture until the oil is completely incorporated and the vinaigrette is smooth and emulsified. Whisk in the parsley and chives. Taste, and adjust the seasoning if necessary.

4. Using tongs or a slotted spoon, carefully remove the leeks from the poaching liquid and set them on a paper towel–lined plate. Allow them to drain and cool slightly before serving, or serve them slightly chilled.

5. Transfer the leeks (1 to 2 pieces per serving) to small salad plates, drizzle with some of the vinaigrette, and serve.

Note: Any remaining vinaigrette will keep, refrigerated in a covered, nonreactive container, for up to 3 days.

4 to 6 servings

ASPARAGUS AND BABY RED RUSSIAN KALE SLAW

People do not usually think about eating asparagus or kale raw, but if you use these ingredients when they are at their freshest and still young and tender, they make a delicious crunchy slaw.

¼ cup finely grated Parmigiano-Reggiano cheese, plus 2 ounces shaved with a vegetable peeler

2 tablespoons freshly squeezed lemon juice

1 teaspoon grated lemon zest

½ teaspoon salt

½ teaspoon freshly ground black pepper

¼ cup extra-virgin olive oil

1 bunch pencil-thin asparagus, sliced on the diagonal into 1-inch pieces

8 ounces (about 1 bunch) baby Red Russian kale, stemmed, leaves rinsed, patted dry, and cut crosswise into thin strips

1. Combine the grated Parmesan, lemon juice, lemon zest, ¼ teaspoon of the salt and ¼ teaspoon of the pepper in a small mixing bowl. Slowly whisk in the olive oil, and set aside.

2. Combine the asparagus and kale in a medium bowl. Season with the remaining ¼ teaspoon salt and ¼ teaspoon pepper, and mix well. Add the shaved Parmesan, toss with the dressing, and let stand for at least 10 minutes.

3. Toss the salad again, and serve. This is best enjoyed at room temperature.

4 servings

SAUTÉED RAMPS WITH APPLE-SMOKED BACON

Ramps are shoots that emerge from the forest floor in early spring. In appearance they resemble green onions, but their flavor is really more of a cross between onion and garlic. Should you be so lucky as to run across freshly foraged ramps in your travels, try them! They are delicious and a real tease for the senses while cooking. We enjoy them crisp-tender after just a quick sauté, but if you prefer them to be more tender, see the note below.

6 ounces thick-sliced applewood-smoked bacon, julienned

2 pounds ramps, rinsed, roots trimmed and sliced ¼ inch thick on the diagonal, leaves roughly chopped

Salt and freshly ground black pepper to taste

1. Heat a large nonstick sauté pan over medium-high heat. Add the bacon and cook until it is just crisp, 5 to 6 minutes. Using a slotted spoon, transfer the bacon to a paper towel–lined plate to drain.

2. Add the ramp bottoms to the bacon fat and cook until nicely browned and caramelized, stirring as necessary, 6 to 8 minutes. During the last 30 seconds of cooking, add the ramp leaves and stir to combine well. (If necessary, cook the ramps in batches and toss the whole batch together before serving.) Season with salt and pepper to taste (depending on the bacon you use, you may not need any additional salt).

3. Transfer to a serving dish, top with the crispy bacon, and serve.

4 servings

Note: If ramps are unavailable in your area, substitute an equal amount of spring onions. And if you would prefer your cooked ramps to be more tender, simply add 1½ to 2 cups chicken broth after sautéing and simmer until the broth has completely evaporated; then allow the ramps to brown before removing them from the pan, 8 to 10 minutes in total.

ASPARAGUS FLAN

The season for asparagus lasts roughly from March to June, depending on where you live. When choosing asparagus, look for spears that are dark green, with firm, round stalks that are not dried out. The tips should be dark green or purple and tightly closed. I like to use medium-size asparagus for this flan, but use whatever size you can find that is very fresh and tender.

1 pound asparagus, tough ends trimmed

1 medium onion, finely chopped

2 tablespoons olive oil

1 teaspoon finely grated lemon zest

2 teaspoons chopped fresh tarragon leaves

3 large eggs

1¼ cups heavy cream

⅓ cup finely grated Parmigiano-Reggiano cheese

¾ teaspoon salt

¼ teaspoon freshly ground white pepper

1 recipe Chive Oil, for serving (page 3, optional)

Edible flowers, for garnish (optional)

1. Fill a medium bowl with ice and cold water, and set it aside.

2. Bring a saucepan of salted water to a boil over high heat. Add the asparagus and cook just until the water returns to a boil. Drain, and immediately submerge the asparagus in the ice water. When it has cooled, drain the spears again, and then chop them crosswise into ½-inch pieces.

3. Preheat the oven to 325°F. Lightly coat the inside of six ½-cup ramekins with nonstick vegetable cooking spray.

4. Combine the asparagus, onion, and olive oil in a large, heavy skillet, and cook over medium heat until the onion is translucent, about 6 minutes. Add the lemon zest and the tarragon, and transfer the mixture to a food processor. Process until very smooth. If there are still some tough fibers after pureeing, pass the mixture through a fine-mesh sieve.

5. Transfer the pureed asparagus mixture to a mixing bowl, and whisk in the eggs, heavy cream, Parmesan, salt, and pepper. Divide the mixture evenly among the prepared ramekins, and place the ramekins in a large baking dish or small roasting pan. Add enough

hot water to reach halfway up the sides of the ramekins, and bake, uncovered, until the flans are set, 25 to
30 minutes. Transfer the ramekins to a wire rack to
cool slightly.

6. When the flans have cooled slightly, run the tip of
a paring knife around the edge of each flan, and turn
the flans out onto serving plates. Garnish each flan
with a little of the Chive Oil and the edible flowers, if
desired. The flans are equally delicious served hot,
warm, or at room temperature.

6 servings

ROASTED GARLIC SOUP

This soup has a lot of depth and complexity; full-bodied flavors come together from the onions, leeks, and roasted garlic. The bread cubes serve to further thicken the soup, but don't be afraid to skip this ingredient should you prefer a thinner soup.

2 tablespoons unsalted butter

4 ounces pancetta, chopped

2 medium leeks (white portions only), well rinsed in several changes of water and finely chopped (about 1¼ cups)

1 cup chopped onions

¼ teaspoon salt, plus more if needed

¼ teaspoon freshly ground white pepper, plus more if needed

1 teaspoon chopped fresh thyme leaves

¾ cup Roasted Garlic (recipe follows)

¼ cup dry white wine

2 quarts chicken or vegetable stock, or canned low-sodium chicken or vegetable broth

½ cup cubed rustic Italian bread (or more if desired)

½ cup heavy cream

2 tablespoons chopped fresh parsley leaves

1 tablespoon freshly squeezed lemon juice

Chopped fresh chives, for garnish

1. Melt the butter in a large pot over medium-high heat. Add the pancetta and cook until the fat is rendered, about 4 minutes. Add the leeks, onions, salt, pepper, and thyme, and cook, stirring, until the vegetables are very soft but not colored, 5 to 6 minutes. Add the roasted garlic, stir well to incorporate, and cook until fragrant, 1 to 2 minutes. Add the wine and bring it to a boil. Cook, stirring, until the wine has nearly completely evaporated, about 2 minutes. Add the stock and bring to a boil. Then reduce the heat and simmer, stirring occasionally, until the vegetables are very soft and the soup is slightly thickened, 20 to 25 minutes.

2. Add the bread cubes to the soup to thicken, as desired. When the bread is soft, puree the soup in a blender or use a handheld immersion blender. Return the pureed soup to the pot. Add the cream, parsley, and lemon juice, and simmer for 5 minutes. Adjust the seasoning if needed.

3. Ladle the soup into bowls, garnish with chopped chives, and serve hot.

About 2 quarts, 4 to 6 servings

ROASTED GARLIC

12 ounces garlic (about 5 large heads)

2 tablespoons extra-virgin olive oil

¼ teaspoon salt

⅛ teaspoon freshly ground black pepper

1. Preheat the oven to 350°F. Cut a piece of aluminum foil to measure approximately 12 × 8 inches.

2. Slice the top quarter off each head of garlic, and place the garlic, cut side up, on one side of the piece of foil. Drizzle the oil over the garlic, and sprinkle with the salt and pepper. Fold the other side of the foil over, and seal on all sides to form an airtight pouch. Transfer the pouch to a baking sheet, and roast in the oven until the cloves are soft and golden brown, about 1 hour.

3. Remove the pouch from the oven and let it sit until the garlic is cool enough to handle. Then squeeze each head of garlic, gently pressing it with your fingers to expel the soft cloves into a bowl. Stir the garlic with a rubber spatula to blend it thoroughly. Use as needed, or store in an airtight container in the refrigerator for up to 2 weeks.

Note: If you don't need 5 whole heads of roasted garlic, simply use as many as you need and follow the method here, drizzling with just enough olive oil to coat the top cut edges of the garlic and season lightly with salt and pepper.

Generous ¾ cup

EMERIL'S ROASTED BEET SALAD WITH WALNUT DRESSING AND CHEESE CRISPS

The intensely colored ruby red and golden beets sparkle like the little jewels they are in this salad.

3 to 4 small red and/or golden beets, tops removed, washed

½ cup plus 2 tablespoons olive oil

3 tablespoons water

½ teaspoon salt, plus more for seasoning

¼ teaspoon freshly ground black pepper, plus more for seasoning

¼ cup sherry vinegar or Banyuls vinegar (see Note)

1 tablespoon finely chopped shallot

1 tablespoon honey

¼ teaspoon Dijon mustard

½ cup grapeseed or olive oil

½ cup chopped toasted walnuts

1 teaspoon minced fresh tarragon leaves

1 bunch baby dandelion greens, stems removed, leaves rinsed and cut into bite-size pieces (about 6 cups or 6 ounces of greens)

1 bunch rainbow chard, stems removed, leaves rinsed and cut into bite-size pieces

Cheese Crisps (recipe follows)

1. Preheat the oven to 350°F.

2. Cut a piece of aluminum foil about 12 inches square. On one half of the square, place the beets, 2 tablespoons olive oil, water, ¼ teaspoon of the salt, and ⅛ teaspoon of the pepper. Fold the opposite side of the foil over to cover the beets, and seal all the edges tightly to form a packet. Place the packet on a baking sheet, transfer it to the oven, and cook until the beets are tender, about 45 minutes. (The beets are done when a paring knife is easily inserted into the middle.) Remove the packet from the oven and set it aside, unopened, for about 10 minutes.

3. Remove the beets from the foil packet. When the beets are cool enough to handle, gently rub off the skin, using a paper towel. Slice the beets into ⅛-inch-thick rounds (use a mandoline if you have one), and set aside.

4. Combine the vinegar, shallot, honey, mustard, remaining ¼ teaspoon salt, and remaining ⅛ teaspoon pepper in a blender, and mix well. While the blender is still running, add the oil in a slow, steady stream, blending until the vinaigrette is emulsified. Transfer the dressing to a mixing bowl, and stir in the walnuts and tarragon.

5. Place the dandelion greens and the chard in a large bowl. Pour 2 tablespoons (or more to taste) of the

dressing over the greens, and season with a pinch of salt and pepper. Toss to coat. In a separate mixing bowl, toss the sliced beets in 1 tablespoon of the dressing, and season with a pinch of salt and pepper.

6. Divide the greens among four to six serving plates, and garnish with the sliced beets and the Cheese Crisps. If desired, spoon more dressing over each salad.

Note: Banyuls vinegar is made from Banyuls wine, which is a fortified wine from southern France and is considered to be the French version of port. Banyuls vinegar has a sweet and nutty flavor, which is generally thought to be milder than red wine vinegar or balsamic vinegar. It tastes something like a cross between balsamic vinegar and sherry vinegar and either can be used as a good substitute. Banyuls vinegar can be found in specialty markets.

4 to 6 servings

CHEESE CRISPS

Cheese crisps can be made from most hard cheeses such as Parmigiano-Reggiano, Montasio, and Asiago. They make easy snacks that can be spiced up with dried herbs and spices. Cheese crisps make a fine accompaniment to soups and salads or they can be served on their own with cocktails.

¾ cup shredded hard sheep's milk cheese, such as Bianco Sardo

1. Preheat the oven to 350°F. Line a baking sheet with a Silpat, or parchment paper.

2. Spacing them 1 to 2 inches apart, place 1-tablespoon mounds of the cheese on the Silpat. Place the baking sheet in the oven and cook until the cheese melts and turns golden brown, about 7 minutes.

3. Remove from the oven and set aside to cool on the baking sheet. Use the crisps as a garnish for soups and salads.

About 12 crisps

CREAMY TURNIP SOUP

This soup highlights the flavor of farm-fresh turnips, an often underrated vegetable in my book. Look for small, firm, young turnips; they will be sweet and tender. Though we call for a mix of chicken and vegetable stock here, either one alone would really work just fine, so use what you prefer and whatever is available.

2 tablespoons unsalted butter

1¼ cups chopped onions

½ cup chopped parsnip or carrot

3 tablespoons minced celery

1 teaspoon minced garlic

4 to 6 sprigs fresh thyme, tied together in a bundle

2 pounds small turnips, peeled and diced

3 cups chicken stock or canned low-sodium chicken broth

1 cup vegetable stock or canned low-sodium vegetable broth

1¼ teaspoons kosher salt

¾ teaspoon freshly ground black pepper

½ cup heavy cream

Sour cream, for garnish

Chopped fresh chives, for garnish

1. Melt the butter in a large saucepan over medium-high heat. Add the onions, parsnip, and celery, and cook until the vegetables are lightly caramelized around the edges, 4 to 6 minutes.

2. Add the garlic and the thyme bundle and cook, stirring, until the garlic is fragrant, 1 to 2 minutes.

3. Add the turnips, both stocks, salt, and pepper, and bring to a boil. Then reduce the heat so that the soup just simmers, and cook until the turnips are very tender, 20 to 25 minutes.

4. Remove the thyme bundle and add the heavy cream. Using an immersion blender (or in batches in a blender), puree the soup until it is very smooth.

5. Rewarm the soup if necessary. Serve it in small bowls, garnished with a dollop of sour cream and a pinch of chives.

Note: Please use caution when blending hot liquids; blend only small amounts at a time, with the blender tightly covered and a kitchen towel held over the top.

1½ quarts, 4 to 6 servings

CELERY ROOT WITH FRESH HERBS AND MUSTARD DRESSING

Ahhh, the wonders of celeriac. It makes a wonderful soup (simmered, pureed, and finished with cream), or you can brown it in a pan and braise it in broth until tender, or you can enjoy it tossed with a traditional rémoulade sauce (the flavorful lemon/herb/cornichon mayo) . . . Here it is shredded and tossed fresh with a simple vinaigrette. Enjoy this as you would any traditional coleslaw—good on its own or, hey, with a barbecued pork sandwich. Or use it as the stage for some plump, crispy fried oysters!

2 medium celery roots (celeriac; about 12 ounces each)

1¾ teaspoons salt

1½ tablespoons freshly squeezed lemon juice

1 tablespoon Dijon mustard

2 tablespoons red wine vinegar

½ cup olive oil

¼ teaspoon freshly ground white pepper

¼ cup finely chopped mixed soft herbs, such as parsley, chives, thyme, and marjoram

2 teaspoons minced gherkin or cornichon

1½ tablespoons minced drained nonpareil capers

1. Using a serrated knife, remove the rooted end and the knobby end of the celery roots. Peel them and cut into chunks. Fit a food processor with the fine shredding disk, and shred the celery root. Transfer it to a bowl, toss it with 1½ teaspoons of the salt and the lemon juice, and set aside.

2. Place the mustard and vinegar in a mixing bowl, and while whisking, slowly drizzle in the olive oil to form an emulsion. Season it with the remaining ¼ teaspoon salt and the white pepper. Stir in the herbs, gherkin, and capers. Add the dressing to the celeriac, and toss to combine.

3. Serve immediately or refrigerate in a nonreactive airtight container for up to 2 days.

About 1 quart, 4 to 6 servings

CARROT SALAD

Gorgeous ribbons of fresh carrots are marinated here in a gaaahlicky, gingery, lemony, honey vinaigrette. Light and refreshing.

1 pound carrots, ends trimmed off, peeled

2 tablespoons canola oil

1 teaspoon cumin seeds

1 teaspoon minced fresh ginger

½ teaspoon minced garlic

¼ cup thinly sliced shallot

½ teaspoon finely grated lemon zest

3 tablespoons freshly squeezed lemon juice

1 teaspoon honey

¼ cup olive oil

¼ teaspoon kosher salt, plus ⅛ teaspoon if needed

¼ teaspoon crushed red pepper

1 tablespoon chopped fresh parsley or mint leaves, or a combination

1. Holding a carrot over a medium bowl, create ribbons by running a vegetable peeler along the length. You will have wider ribbons if you keep the carrot steady and peel two opposing sides until you are left with a core. (Discard the cores or save them in your freezer for stock, chop them and add them to a soup, or add them to your compost pile.)

2. Fill a medium bowl with ice and cold water, and set it aside.

3. Bring a medium pot of salted water to a boil, add the carrot ribbons, and cook for 10 seconds. Drain, and immediately plunge the carrots into the bowl of ice water to stop the cooking. Once they are completely cooled, remove the carrot ribbons from the ice bath, lay them on a kitchen towel, and gently roll them up in the towel so that they are thoroughly dried.

4. Make the vinaigrette: Combine the canola oil, cumin seeds, ginger, and garlic in a small sauté pan, set it over low heat, and heat until the garlic sizzles, about 30 seconds. Remove from the heat. Transfer the mixture to a mortar, and grind it with a pestle. Transfer this mixture to a small bowl, and add the shallot, lemon zest, lemon juice, and honey. Slowly drizzle in the olive oil, whisking to combine. Add the ¼ teaspoon salt and the crushed red pepper. Stir in the parsley.

5. Combine the carrot ribbons with the vinaigrette, and set the salad aside to marinate for at least 10 minutes before serving. Taste, and season with the remaining ⅛ teaspoon salt if desired.

4 servings

CARAMELIZED CANE SYRUP SWEET POTATOES

These are so addictive! The Louisiana cane syrup gives the sweet potatoes a unique flavor, but if you can't find Steen's, you could certainly substitute a mixture of molasses and dark corn syrup.

About 3 pounds sweet potatoes, peeled and sliced crosswise into ½-inch-thick rounds

2 tablespoons canola or grapeseed oil

½ teaspoon salt

4 tablespoons (½ stick) butter, melted

¼ cup cane syrup (we recommend Steen's)

½ cup packed dark brown sugar

1 cup pecan pieces

1. Preheat the oven to 400°F.

2. Combine the sweet potatoes with the oil and salt in a mixing bowl, and toss to coat well. Place the sweet potatoes on a baking sheet and arrange them in a single layer. Transfer to the oven and cook until they begin to caramelize and soften, about 30 minutes.

3. Meanwhile, combine all the remaining ingredients in a small mixing bowl.

4. Transfer the potatoes to a casserole dish. Pour the syrup mixture over them, and using a spatula, toss to coat well. Return the casserole to the oven and continue to cook, carefully stirring once, until the potatoes are caramelized and tender, about 30 minutes. Serve hot.

4 to 6 servings

SUNCHOKES, CARROTS, AND PARSNIPS WITH BACON

The sunchoke, also known as the Jerusalem artichoke or earth apple, is indigenous to North America and was cultivated first by Native Americans. In this recipe they are roasted along with carrots and parsnips and tossed with an apple cider vinaigrette. There's lots of flexibility here: you can prepare this dish with any plentiful local root vegetable you like, such as turnip, rutabaga, salsify, baby beet, or potato. Delicious.

2 pounds sunchokes, scrubbed well and cut into 1-inch wedges

1 pound carrots, cut into 2-inch diagonal pieces

1 pound parsnips, cut into 2-inch diagonal pieces

¾ cup olive oil

¾ teaspoon salt

¾ teaspoon freshly ground black pepper

4 ounces sliced bacon, cut into ½-inch pieces (about ⅔ cup)

6 shallots, thinly sliced (about ⅔ cup)

1 teaspoon minced garlic

2 tablespoons chopped fresh parsley leaves

¾ teaspoon sugar

¼ cup cider vinegar

1. Preheat the oven to 500°F.

2. In a medium bowl, combine the sunchokes, carrots, parsnips, ¼ cup of the olive oil, the salt, and the pepper. Transfer the vegetables to a rimmed baking sheet and roast in the oven for 20 minutes, until lightly caramelized and tender, stirring once midway through cooking.

3. While the vegetables are roasting, place the bacon in a small sauté pan over medium-high heat and cook for 2 minutes. Add the shallots, reduce the heat to low, and cook for 5 more minutes, or until the bacon fat is rendered and the shallots are lightly caramelized. Drain, discarding all but 1 tablespoon of the fat from the pan.

4. Transfer the bacon/shallot mixture to a medium mixing bowl. Add the garlic, parsley, and sugar, and whisk to combine. Whisk in the vinegar. Slowly whisk in the remaining ½ cup olive oil, and set aside.

5. Transfer the roasted vegetables to the mixing bowl, and toss with the vinaigrette to combine. Serve warm.

4 to 6 servings

BEET "CAVIAR"

Beets are one of my favorite root vegetables. They come in a wonderful array of colors and sizes, from golden yellow to candy-stripe. The whole plant can be utilized: the tops can be cooked just like any other hearty green and the beet root can be eaten raw, roasted, boiled, or shredded. In this recipe the texture of finely chopped beets combined with poppy seeds is reminiscent of caviar. The "caviar" is served over baby greens here, but it would also be a nice topping for canapés served on crostini, garnished with a dollop of crème fraîche.

1 pound beets, roasted until tender (see page 172) and peeled

¼ cup freshly squeezed orange juice

2 tablespoons white wine vinegar

2 tablespoons minced shallot

2 tablespoons poppy seeds

1 teaspoon grated orange zest

1 teaspoon salt

½ teaspoon freshly ground white pepper

10 ounces baby arugula, rinsed and spun dry

3 tablespoons Chive Oil (page 3), for serving

1. Using a mandoline, slice the beets to ⅛-inch thickness. Then cut the beets into a fine brunoise (very fine dice, about ⅛ inch square). Set aside.

2. Combine the orange juice, white wine vinegar, shallot, poppy seeds, orange zest, salt, and pepper in a small bowl.

3. In a medium bowl, combine the beets with two-thirds of the vinaigrette. In a separate bowl, toss the arugula with the remaining vinaigrette.

4. Divide the arugula evenly among six plates. Then mound the beets on top of the greens. Drizzle each plate with Chive Oil, and serve immediately.

Note: The beets can be roasted 1 day in advance.

6 servings

TURNIP AND RADISH SLAW WITH JUMBO LUMP CRABMEAT AND CHIVE OIL

Thinly sliced turnips and radishes are lightly tossed with a champagne vinaigrette, then topped with creamy, succulent crabmeat and drizzled with Chive Oil. Elegant, and simply marvelous.

. . . .

1 tablespoon minced shallot

1 tablespoon finely chopped fresh chives

2 teaspoons Dijon mustard

2 teaspoons chopped fresh tarragon leaves

2 teaspoons chopped fresh chervil leaves

2 teaspoons chopped fresh parsley leaves

1 teaspoon chopped drained nonpareil capers

1 teaspoon chopped cornichon

⅓ cup champagne vinegar

¾ cup grapeseed oil

Salt, to taste

Freshly ground white pepper, to taste

1 turnip (about the size of a baseball), peeled and julienned

1 small bunch radishes (about 6), julienned

¼ cup mayonnaise, store-bought or homemade (see page 153)

1 tablespoon freshly squeezed lemon juice

⅛ teaspoon cayenne pepper

1 pound jumbo lump crabmeat, picked over for shells and cartilage

1 recipe Chive Oil (page 3)

Chive blossoms, for garnish (optional)

1. In a small bowl, combine the shallot, chives, mustard, tarragon, chervil, parsley, capers, cornichon, vinegar, and grapeseed oil. Season with salt and pepper to taste.

2. In a medium mixing bowl, toss ¼ cup of the vinaigrette with the turnip and radishes. Season with salt and pepper to taste.

3. Combine the mayonnaise, lemon juice, and cayenne in a medium bowl. Add ¼ cup of the vinaigrette and mix well. Add the crabmeat and toss to coat.

4. To serve, divide the turnip-radish slaw among four to six chilled plates. Spoon the crabmeat on the top of the slaw, trying to keep the crabmeat lumps as intact as possible. Drizzle the Chive Oil around each plate, and garnish with chive blossoms if desired.

4 to 6 servings

FRESH HORSERADISH CREAM SAUCE

Everybody will love eating this spooned over a beef rib roast or spread on a sandwich, but making it is not for the meek. I'm tellin' ya, grating fresh horseradish is like standing over a bowl of wasabi and breathing in. You will get equally good results either grating by hand on the side of a cheese grater or, with less tears, using the fine grater attachment on your food processor.

3 cups heavy cream

1½ cups finely grated fresh horseradish (from about 8 ounces horseradish root)

6 tablespoons finely chopped shallot

4 teaspoons minced garlic

4 teaspoons Dijon mustard

2 teaspoons kosher salt

½ teaspoon freshly ground white or black pepper (optional)

1. Combine all of the ingredients in a medium saucepan, and bring to a boil. Then reduce the heat to a simmer, and cook, stirring occasionally, until the sauce is thick enough to coat the back of a spoon, about 12 minutes.

2. Remove from the heat and serve warm. (The sauce can be refrigerated and served cold on a sandwich.) The sauce will keep, refrigerated in an airtight, nonreactive container, for up to 2 weeks.

2 cups

MASHED RUTABAGA

If you're in the mood for a mash but want something other than the standard potato variation, why not try the frequently forgotten rutabaga? Rutabaga has a slightly bitter, turnip-like flavor that (also like turnips) sweetens once cooked. We enjoyed this roughly mashed so that some lumps still remained, but go ahead and mash according to your liking.

5 pounds rutabaga, peeled and cut into 1-inch chunks

1 cup heavy cream

1½ teaspoons chopped fresh thyme leaves

2 tablespoons butter, diced

2 tablespoons chopped fresh chives

Salt and freshly ground black pepper, to taste

1. Fill a large pot with salted water, and add the rutabaga. Make sure there is enough water to cover the rutabaga by at least an inch. Bring to a rolling boil. Then reduce the heat to a simmer, cover the pot, and simmer until the rutabaga is completely cooked through and very tender, 30 to 35 minutes.

2. During the last 5 minutes that the rutabaga is cooking, combine the heavy cream and thyme in a small saucepan and place over medium heat. Cook until the mixture is just warmed through. Remove from the heat and set aside.

3. Drain the rutabaga in a colander, discarding the cooking liquid. Return the rutabaga to the pot. Begin mashing the rutabaga with a hand masher, adding the warmed cream little by little. Add the butter and continue mashing until is completely melted and mixed through. Add the chives and fold them into the mashed rutabaga. Season with salt and pepper to taste, and serve hot.

4 to 6 servings

SWEET POTATO RAVIOLI WITH SAGE BROWN BUTTER

The sweet potato filling here is the perfect vehicle for the luscious nutty browned butter. Top it all with crispy sage, and you've got a textural party going on. The key to getting the pasta right lies all in the kneading: follow the instructions and knead the dough for 10 solid minutes. Doing so will activate the gluten in the dough for the perfect toothsome texture.

Olive oil, for drizzling

1 pound (2 small or 1 very large) sweet potatoes

2 tablespoons mascarpone cheese

Salt and freshly ground white pepper

¾ cup cake flour

¾ cup all-purpose flour

2 eggs

2 tablespoons olive oil

Water, as needed

8 tablespoons (1 stick) unsalted butter, cut into large uniform chunks

16 fresh sage leaves

1. Preheat the oven to 350°F.

2. Drizzle olive oil lightly over the sweet potatoes and rub to coat them. Place the potatoes on a baking sheet and bake, turning them over midway through, until tender, about 1 hour. Remove from the oven and set aside until cool enough to handle.

3. Peel the potatoes and discard the skin. Place the sweet potato flesh in a medium mixing bowl, and mash with a fork or the back of a spoon until smooth. Add the mascarpone cheese, and using a wooden spoon, mix until you can no longer see chunks of the mascarpone. Season with salt and pepper to taste, and set aside until ready to use.

4. Make the ravioli dough: Combine the cake flour and all-purpose flour in a bowl, and whisk them together. Form a small well in the mixture, add the eggs and olive oil to the well, and gradually combine until the dough comes together. If the dough seems a little dry, add very small amounts of water at a time until the dough seems smooth and supple and will come together into a smooth ball. Transfer the dough to a clean work surface, and knead it for at least 10 minutes. Form the dough into a ball and wrap it well with plastic wrap. Set it aside to rest at room temperature for at least 30 minutes, or refrigerate up to overnight. (Return to room temperature before rolling out.)

5. Cut the dough into 4 portions. Working with one portion at a time, flatten the dough into a disk with the palm of your hand. Beginning with the widest setting on a pasta machine, roll the dough through the machine, folding the pasta into thirds after each "run." Run it through about two times at each setting, decreasing the settings until you get to the thinnest setting, at which point you can just run the pasta through once. Repeat with the remaining portions of dough. You should have 4 long sheets of very thin pasta dough.

6. Form the ravioli by spacing small mounds of the sweet potato filling (about 1 teaspoon each) onto one of the pasta sheets in rows, leaving about an inch of space between the mounds and around the sides for sealing. Run a wet finger around the edges of the filling mounds, and then top with one of the unfilled pasta sheets. Ease the pasta down around the mounds, pressing down around the filling so that each ravioli is sealed. Cut the ravioli out with a round cookie cutter (about 2¼ inches) or with a rolling pasta cutter. Crimp the edges with the tines of a fork, if desired, to further ensure that the ravioli are sealed. Repeat until you have used up all of the filling and pasta.

7. Fill a large pot with salted water and bring it to a boil. Place the ravioli in the boiling water (in batches, if necessary) and cook until al dente, 1 to 2 minutes. Remove the ravioli with a slotted spoon and place them on a paper towel–lined plate to drain. Cover lightly with a towel to keep warm.

8. Heat a sauté pan over medium-high heat, and when it is hot, add the butter and let it melt in one spot (do not move the pan). When the butter has begun to brown around the edges and smells nutty, pick up the sauté pan and swirl it to keep the melted butter from burning and to melt the remaining butter. Add the sage leaves and reduce the heat to medium-low. Cook until the leaves are crispy, 1 to 2 minutes. Season with salt and white pepper to taste.

9. Divide the ravioli among four to six shallow bowls or plates. Drizzle the brown butter on top, and garnish with the crispy sage leaves. Serve immediately.

40 raviolis, 4 to 6 servings

winter fruits

ORANGECELLO

Limoncello, a richly lemon-scented liqueur produced mainly in southern Italy, is traditionally served chilled as an after-dinner digestif. It is fairly easy to make at home and can be made with a variety of lemons to produce slightly different results. I thought it would be fun to try to make this traditional drink with oranges instead, and the results are out of sight.

8 navel oranges

1 bottle (750 ml) Everclear or other neutral high-proof alcohol

2½ cups sugar

6 cups water

1. Remove the orange zest with a Microplane zester or a vegetable peeler, being careful to avoid any white pith. Set the oranges aside for another use.

2. Put the zest and the alcohol in a glass jar, and cover it with a tight-fitting lid. Set it aside in a cool, dark place for 4 days, until the zest has turned pale and the alcohol has an orange color.

3. Strain the alcohol through a fine-mesh sieve into a clean bowl. Discard the solids.

4. Combine the sugar and the water in a medium saucepan, and stir over medium heat until the sugar dissolves and the syrup is clear. Do not allow it to boil. Remove from the heat and let cool.

5. Once the syrup is cool, add it to the strained alcohol, and stir to combine. Pour the orange-infused liqueur into clean bottles, and seal them with corks or screw tops. Set aside for 2 weeks at cool room temperature to allow the liqueur to mellow.

6. Chill before serving.

10 cups

SATSUMA VINAIGRETTE

Satsumas, like tangerines, are part of the mandarin orange family. Small and sweet, they are prized for their flavor. In southeastern Louisiana, citrus groves flourish with specialties such as satsumas, sweet navel oranges, Meyer lemons, and tangerines. Citrus vinaigrettes are versatile—they can be used not only on salads but also drizzled over sautéed fish or grilled chicken. This recipe can be adapted to use any variety of mandarin.

4 satsumas

1 tablespoon white wine vinegar

2 teaspoons freshly squeezed
  lemon juice

1½ teaspoons finely chopped
  shallot

⅔ cup canola oil

Salt and freshly ground black
  pepper, to taste

1. Using a Microplane zester, grate 1 teaspoon zest from one of the satsumas. Then cut away all the peel from the satsumas, leaving them free of any white pith. Working over a bowl, segment the satsumas by slicing along the membranes on both sides of each segment. Use the edge of the knife to help release the segments into the bowl. Squeeze the membranes over a separate nonreactive bowl to release any remaining juices; you should have ¼ cup.

2. Add the vinegar, lemon juice, shallot, and satsuma zest to the bowl containing the juice. While whisking, add the oil in a slow, steady stream until the dressing is emulsified. Season with salt and pepper to taste. Stir in the satsuma segments.

1¹/₂ cups

ORANGE CURD

Five simple farm-fresh ingredients—a luscious indulgence. We love this with the Rosemary Buttermilk Scones on page 16.

1½ cups freshly squeezed orange juice

6 large egg yolks

6 tablespoons sugar

2 teaspoons finely grated orange zest

4 tablespoons (½ stick) cold unsalted butter, cut into 8 pieces

1. Pour the orange juice into a small saucepan, and cook over medium-high heat until reduced to ½ cup. (Have a liquid measure nearby so that you can check the volume as necessary.) Set the reduction aside to cool slightly.

2. Fill a small pot one-third of the way with water, and bring it to a boil.

3. In a medium metal bowl, whisk together the egg yolks, sugar, and orange zest. While whisking, slowly add the reduced orange juice until completely incorporated. Set the bowl over the pot of boiling water, and reduce the heat to medium-low. Whisk constantly for 6 to 7 minutes, or until the curd thickens and holds its shape when stirred. (You can also do this in a double boiler.) Remove the bowl from the heat and gradually stir in the butter.

4. Set a metal bowl into a larger bowl of ice water, and strain the curd through a fine-mesh sieve into the smaller bowl. Stir the curd occasionally until it is cool, about 5 minutes. Transfer the curd to a small container, cover with plastic wrap, and refrigerate until well chilled. Use within 1 week.

2 cups

ORANGE CRANBERRY SAUCE

Cranberries are one of the few fruits native to the northeastern United States, growing wild in bogs and swamps. Cranberries have become a staple at holiday meals, especially Thanksgiving. This is my kicked-up version of cranberry sauce.

1 bag (12 ounces) cranberries

Grated zest and juice of 2 oranges

¼ cup ruby port

¾ cup sugar, or more to taste

½ teaspoon ground cinnamon

½ teaspoon ground cardamom

1 cup toasted pecans or walnuts

1. Combine the cranberries, orange zest and juice, port, sugar, cinnamon, and cardamom in a small saucepan, and bring to a boil. Reduce the heat to a simmer and cook, stirring occasionally, until the cranberries are tender and the sauce has thickened, about 10 minutes.

2. Taste, and add more sugar if desired. Stir in the nuts and set aside to cool. Serve at room temperature. (The sauce can be made up to 3 days in advance and stored in an airtight container in the refrigerator until ready to serve.)

2 cups

EMERIL'S WHOLE ROASTED DUCK WITH CANDIED KUMQUATS

This basic, foolproof method for a crisp and flavorful farm-raised domestic duck is the perfect way to showcase the uniquely delicious flavor of kumquats. By piercing the skin and poaching the duck first, much of the excess fat is removed, affording a crispy skin and a juicy roasted duck. The remaining poaching liquid is rich and flavorful and can be frozen for later use in soups, stews, and sauces. Feel free to make the simple kumquat sauce to serve alongside roasted pork, too.

4 to 5 quarts duck stock, chicken stock, or water

Two 5½-pound ducks, innards, wing tips, and extra fat removed

1 pound kumquats, sliced ¼ inch thick

1½ cups water

1½ cups sugar

1 cinnamon stick (3 inches long)

¼ teaspoon whole allspice berries

½ vanilla bean, seeds scraped out and reserved

1 teaspoon kosher salt

¾ teaspoon freshly ground black pepper

1. Bring the stock to a simmer in a large stockpot.

2. While the stock is heating, use the tip of a small sharp knife to pierce the ducks' skin in a number of places without piercing the meat.

3. Carefully lower the ducks into the simmering broth, fully submerging them. Place a heatproof plate or a small pot on top of the ducks to keep them submerged, and simmer for 45 minutes.

4. While the ducks are poaching, place the kumquats in a 1-quart saucepan and add enough water to cover them. Bring to a medium simmer and cook for about 5 minutes. Drain, and discard the cooking liquid. Set the kumquats aside.

5. In the same saucepan, combine the 1½ cups water with the sugar, cinnamon stick, and allspice berries, and bring to a boil. Reduce the heat to a simmer, and add the vanilla pod and the scraped seeds. Simmer for about 5 minutes. Then add the kumquats and cook until they are tender and slightly translucent, about 8 minutes. Remove the pan from the heat, and transfer the sauce to a heatproof, nonreactive bowl. The sauce may be served warm or at room temperature.

6. Preheat the oven to 500°F.

7. Carefully remove the ducks from the poaching liquid and transfer them to a rack set in a shallow roasting pan. Using paper towels, pat the ducks dry. Season them with the salt and pepper. Place the pan in the oven and roast the ducks for 30 minutes.

8. Remove the ducks from the oven and let them rest for 15 minutes before serving. Pass the kumquat sauce at the table.

4 to 6 servings

MEYER LEMON PUDDING CAKES

Meyer lemons, with their slight orange hue, originally hailed from China, where lemons were crossed with mandarin oranges. Meyer lemons have become a favorite of chefs because of their sweet, almost floral, flavor and deep aroma. They are a great alternative to lemons, even though they are considerably less acidic. These little pudding cakes really let their flavor shine.

. . . .

2 tablespoons plus 1½ teaspoons unsalted butter, at room temperature

1 cup sugar

3 teaspoons finely grated Meyer lemon zest

3 large eggs, separated, at room temperature

¼ cup all-purpose flour

½ cup Meyer lemon juice

1 cup buttermilk

Confectioners' sugar, for garnish

1. Preheat the oven to 350°F.

2. Using the 1½ teaspoons butter, butter six ¾-cup ramekins. Place the ramekins in a large baking dish or roasting pan, and set it aside.

3. In a mixing bowl, cream together the sugar, remaining 2 tablespoons butter, and lemon zest. Add the egg yolks, one at a time, beating well after each addition. Stir in the flour. Gradually add the lemon juice (don't worry if the mixture looks curdled or appears to be separating). Stir in the buttermilk.

4. In a separate bowl, beat the egg whites until they just hold stiff peaks. Gently fold the egg whites into the yolk mixture in three additions. (Tip: Fold gently with a large whisk to initiate blending, then proceed with a large rubber spatula.) Do not overmix; the mixture will appear thin.

5. Divide the batter evenly among the prepared ramekins, and add enough hot water to the baking dish to reach halfway up the sides of the ramekins. Bake until the pudding cakes are golden brown on top, puffed, and lightly firm to the touch, 35 to 40 minutes. (If the cakes begin to brown too much before they are done, cover loosely with a piece of aluminum foil.) Remove

the baking dish from the oven and transfer the ramekins to a wire rack to cool slightly.

6. When the cakes have cooled a bit, dust them lightly
with confectioners' sugar. Serve warm.

6 servings

RED GRAPEFRUIT SORBET

You're basically eating a fresh, frozen grapefruit when you're eating this sorbet. However, it's extra-special because it has a bit of kick to it. The black pepper complements the sweetness, but it doesn't hit you right away. Instead, it lingers lightly at the back of the tongue.

1¼ cups sugar

1¼ cups water

1 teaspoon grated grapefruit zest

2 cups freshly squeezed red
   grapefruit juice

2 tablespoons freshly squeezed
   lemon juice

½ teaspoon freshly ground black
   pepper

1. Combine the sugar, water, and grapefruit zest in a medium saucepan, and bring to a boil over medium-high heat, stirring occasionally until the sugar dissolves. Remove the pan from the heat and set it aside to steep for 5 minutes.

2. Stir in the grapefruit juice and lemon juice. Strain the mixture through a fine-mesh sieve into a bowl. Stir in the black pepper, and set it aside to cool. (It will cool faster if you set the container in a bowl of ice water and stir it intermittently.)

3. Cover and refrigerate the sorbet base until it is thoroughly chilled, about 4 hours or up to overnight.

4. Process the sorbet in an ice cream machine according to the manufacturer's directions. Transfer it to a freezerproof container, cover, and freeze until ready to serve.

About 1¼ quarts, 4 to 6 servings

from the mill

CREAMY SPICED RICE PUDDING

The rice you use in this pudding will make all the difference, so for the best results, look for a fragrant heirloom long-grain variety. The rice fields in southwest Louisiana produce some of the best rice around; if you can find Louisiana popcorn rice, by all means, give it a try. The nutty aroma alone is worth the price of admission.

1 cup aromatic long-grain rice, such as Louisiana popcorn rice, Texmati, basmati, or jasmine

1 cup water

1 cinnamon stick (3 inches long)

¼ teaspoon salt

2 pinches ground cardamom

1 pinch ground coriander

4 cups whole milk

¼ cup heavy cream, plus more for serving

6 tablespoons packed light brown sugar, plus more for serving

1. Combine the rice, water, cinnamon stick, salt, cardamom, and coriander in a medium saucepan, and bring to a boil. Stir, cover the pot, and reduce the heat to low. Cook until the water has been absorbed, about 6 minutes.

2. Remove the lid and stir in 2 cups of the milk, the heavy cream, and the brown sugar. Bring to a simmer and cook, uncovered, stirring occasionally, until the rice has absorbed most of the milk and is creamy, about 8 minutes.

3. Add 1 cup of the remaining milk and simmer, stirring frequently, until the rice has once again absorbed the milk and is thick and creamy, about 8 minutes. Add the final 1 cup milk and cook until the rice is completely tender and soft, 8 to 10 minutes, stirring nearly constantly to prevent the rice from sticking to the bottom of the pan. Remove the pan from the heat, cover, and set it aside for 10 to 15 minutes.

4. Serve the rice pudding warm, drizzled with additional heavy cream and sprinkled with brown sugar to taste.

6 servings

FIVE-GRAIN SALAD

There are numerous health benefits to eating whole grains: they are low in fat, high in fiber, and one of nature's superfoods. They have a long culinary history: amaranth and quinoa are American heritage grains that were eaten by the Aztecs and Incas respectively. Today these grains are widely cultivated and prized in the kitchen, not only for their nutritional value but also for their flavor and versatility.

- 2 cups cooked wild rice (cooking directions follow)
- 1 cup cooked amaranth (cooking directions follow)
- 1 cup cooked quinoa (cooking directions follow)
- 1 cup cooked millet (cooking directions follow)
- 1 cup cooked brown Jasmati, brown basmati, or brown jasmine rice (cooked according to the package directions)
- 1 teaspoon grated orange zest
- 1 cup fresh orange segments
- 1 cup diced fennel (small dice)
- ½ cup diced radishes (small dice)
- ½ cup extra-virgin olive oil
- ¼ cup freshly squeezed orange juice
- 3 tablespoons red wine vinegar
- 1 tablespoon chopped fresh fennel fronds
- 1 teaspoon chopped fresh dill
- 1 teaspoon kosher salt
- ¼ teaspoon freshly ground black pepper

Combine all the ingredients in a large bowl. Refrigerate, covered, for at least 1 hour or as long as 3 to 4 days before serving. Remove from the refrigerator and serve at room temperature.

Note: *Whole Grains as a Superfood*

Whole grains retain their bran, which is its fibrous outer layer. Fiber keeps our heart healthy by lowering our cholesterol and blood pressure as well as maintaining stable blood sugar levels. Whole grains as opposed to processed grains have a higher nutrient content and are full of antioxidants. Some studies say that antioxidants combat cancer-causing free radicals in our body.

6 cups, about 6 servings

AMARANTH

1 cup amaranth seeds

1 cup vegetable stock or canned
    low-sodium vegetable broth

Pinch of salt

1. Place a small saucepan over medium-high heat, and add the amaranth. Toast until it begins to pop, 4 to 5 minutes.

2. While the amaranth is cooking, bring the stock to a boil in a medium saucepan.

3. Add the amaranth and the salt to the stock. Cover the pan, reduce the heat, and simmer until all the liquid has been absorbed, 7 minutes.

4. Remove the pan from the heat and set it aside, still covered, to steam for 7 minutes.

5. Pour the amaranth into a bowl and use as desired.

1½ cups

QUINOA

1 cup vegetable stock or canned
    low-sodium vegetable broth

¼ teaspoon salt

⅛ teaspoon freshly ground black
    pepper

½ cup quinoa

1. Combine the stock, salt, and pepper in a medium saucepan and bring to a boil over high heat. Add the quinoa, cover the pan, and reduce the heat. Simmer the quinoa until all the liquid has been absorbed, 12 minutes.

2. Remove the pan from the heat and let it stand, still covered, for 5 minutes.

3. Fluff the quinoa with a fork, and use as desired.

2 cups

MILLET

½ cup hulled millet

1 cup vegetable stock or canned
 low-sodium vegetable broth

Sea salt and freshly ground black
 pepper to taste

1. Place a small saucepan over medium-high heat, and add the millet. Toast until it has a nutty smell, 4 to 5 minutes.

2. As soon as the first grain pops, remove the pan from the heat and pour the millet into a bowl. Add cold water and swirl it to wash the millet. Then pour the millet into a fine-mesh sieve and rinse it under cold running water for another minute or until the water runs clear.

3. Bring the stock to a boil in a medium saucepan. Add the millet and salt and pepper to taste, reduce the heat, and simmer, covered, until all the liquid has been absorbed, 20 minutes.

4. Remove the pan from the heat and let it stand, still covered, for 5 minutes.

5. Fluff the millet with a fork, and use as desired.

2 cups

WILD RICE

½ cup wild rice

1½ cups water

1 tablespoon butter

¼ teaspoon sea salt

1. Combine all the ingredients in a medium saucepan and bring to a boil. Stir, cover the pan, and reduce the heat to a simmer. Cook until all the liquid has been absorbed, 50 to 55 minutes.

2. Remove the pan from the heat and let it stand, covered, for 10 minutes.

3. Fluff the rice with a fork, adjust the seasoning if necessary, and use as desired.

2 cups

GREEN ONION SPOONBREAD

Not much needs to be added to this luscious, moist spoonbread—it is delicious simply with green onions and cheese as an accent. But your imagination can run wild without much risk. Add an abundant herb or another of your favorite ingredients: garlic, crumbled crisp-cooked bacon, corn kernels . . .

3 tablespoons unsalted butter

1 cup plus 3 tablespoons stone-ground cornmeal

1⅔ cups whole milk

⅔ cup heavy cream

⅔ cup buttermilk

1 teaspoon salt

1 teaspoon freshly ground black pepper

4 ounces sharp cheddar cheese, grated

4 eggs, separated

¼ cup finely chopped green onions, green and white parts

1 teaspoon chopped fresh thyme leaves

1 teaspoon baking soda

1 teaspoon baking powder

2 teaspoons sugar

1. Butter a 9×13-inch baking dish with 1 tablespoon of the butter. Add the 3 tablespoons cornmeal to the dish and tilt the dish to coat the bottom and sides with the cornmeal. Set the baking dish aside.

2. Combine the milk, cream, buttermilk, salt, and pepper in a medium saucepan, and bring just to a boil. Whisk in the 1 cup cornmeal and cook, stirring constantly, until the mixture thickens and has the consistency of grits, 1 to 2 minutes. Remove from the heat and immediately transfer the mixture to a heatproof bowl. Stir in the cheese, and set the bowl aside until the mixture is lukewarm, stirring often to prevent a skin from forming on the top, 10 to 15 minutes.

3. Preheat the oven to 350°F.

4. In a small bowl, lightly beat the egg yolks. Then stir the yolks, green onions, thyme, baking soda, and baking powder into the cornmeal mixture.

5. Combine the egg whites and the sugar in a mixing bowl, and beat until stiff peaks form. Fold one-third of the whites into the cornmeal mixture to lighten it. Then gently fold in the remaining whites, taking care not to deflate the whites.

6. Transfer the mixture to the prepared baking dish, and bake until the spoonbread is puffed and golden brown on top, and a knife inserted into the center comes out clean, about 30 minutes. Serve immediately.

8 to 10 servings

QUINOA WITH TOASTED PECANS

The quinoa plant is closely related to Swiss chard, but it's primarily for the seeds that this ancient grainlike crop is cultivated. Not only are they a complete protein but they contain all of the essential amino acids, making them a cherished food. Quinoa has a mild, nutty flavor and a fluffy texture similar to couscous.

2 cups chicken stock or canned low-sodium chicken broth

1 cup quinoa, rinsed

¼ cup chopped pecans

⅓ cup chopped fresh parsley leaves

1 tablespoon olive oil

Salt and freshly ground black pepper

1. Combine the stock and the quinoa in a medium saucepan and bring to a boil. Reduce the heat to a simmer, cover, and cook for 15 to 18 minutes, until the liquid has been absorbed and the grain is tender.

2. Meanwhile, toast the pecans in a small, dry skillet over medium-high heat, stirring frequently, until they are golden brown and fragrant, about 2 minutes. Remove the nuts from the skillet and set them aside.

3. When the quinoa is done, fluff it with a fork and transfer it to a large serving bowl. Stir in the pecans, parsley, and olive oil. Season with salt and pepper to taste, and serve hot.

3 cups, 2 to 4 servings

HOMEMADE PASTA WITH PANCETTA AND CHANTERELLES

Making pasta at home may seem daunting even to an experienced cook, but I assure you that it is not as difficult as it seems—and it's tons of fun, especially if you can get the kids involved. Fresh pasta is usually made with soft wheat flour. For this recipe I used Anson Mills Red Fife bread flour combined with a little cake flour to make a tender dough. Take care when cooking fresh pasta: it cooks more quickly than the dried variety.

For the pasta

¾ cup plus 2 tablespoons soft whole wheat flour, such as Red Fife flour from Anson Mills (see Note), or all-purpose flour

¾ cup plus 2 tablespoons cake flour

2 large eggs

2 tablespoons olive oil

For the sauce

4 ounces pancetta, cut into ¼-inch dice

1 tablespoon extra-virgin olive oil

¼ cup minced shallot

8 ounces fresh chanterelles, stems trimmed, cut into quarters

1½ teaspoons chopped fresh thyme leaves

¾ cup dry white wine

½ cup heavy cream

1 teaspoon sea salt

½ teaspoon freshly ground black pepper

1. Combine the whole wheat flour and the cake flour in a bowl, and whisk together. Create a small well in the flour. Add the eggs and olive oil to the well, and gradually combine until the dough comes together. (If the dough seems a little dry, add very small amounts of water at a time.) Form into a ball with your hands. Transfer the dough to a clean work surface and knead it for at least 10 minutes, until smooth. Form the dough into a ball and wrap it well with plastic wrap. Let it rest at room temperature for at least 30 minutes and up to 1 hour or refrigerate up to overnight. (Allow to return to room temperature before rolling out.)

2. Cut the dough into four portions. Working with one portion at a time, flatten the dough into a disk with the palm of your hand. Beginning with the thickest setting on a pasta machine, roll the pasta once. Then fold the pasta into thirds and roll it through the same setting a second time. The dough should begin to feel more elastic; if not, fold it in half again and roll it through the thickest setting one last time. Then roll the pasta through each setting, changing settings as the dough gets thinner with each roll-through, until you get to the thinnest setting.

Note: Red Fife flour is made from a heritage wheat that was grown in Canada in the mid-nineteenth century by a farmer in Ontario named Dave Fife. Although the wheat seemed to disappear some time around the Great Depression, it has made an enormous resurgence. It is considered to be the finest wheat to use for bread baking because of its rich aroma and flavor. Red Fife flour can be purchased from Anson Mills online.

3. Using the cutting attachment, run the rolled pasta sheets through the blades to cut into noodles of the desired width. Set the pasta to dry on a lightly floured baking sheet, or hang it on a drying rack, while you make the sauce.

4. Heat a 14-inch sauté pan over medium heat. Add the pancetta and cook for 2 to 3 minutes, or until it has rendered most of its fat and is crispy. Use a slotted spoon to transfer the pancetta to a paper towel–lined plate, and set it aside. Add the extra-virgin olive oil and the shallots to the pan, and cook for 1 to 2 minutes, or until the shallots are slightly wilted. Add the chanterelles and the thyme, and sauté, stirring, until the mushrooms are golden brown, 3 minutes. Add the white wine and cook until it has reduced by half, about 4 minutes. Stir in the heavy cream, cover the pan, and simmer for 10 to 12 minutes. Season the sauce with the sea salt and black pepper. Keep it warm.

5. Bring a large pot of generously salted water to a boil. Add the fresh pasta. As soon as the water returns to a boil and the pasta has floated to the top, drain the pasta in a colander, reserving ¼ cup of the cooking liquid.

6. Add the pasta and the reserved cooking liquid to the sauce, and toss well. Adjust the seasoning if necessary, and serve immediately.

4 servings

WILD MUSHROOM RAGOUT OVER CREAMY POLENTA

Wild mushrooms, with their earthy flavor and meaty texture, come into season in both spring and fall. Mushrooms with such interesting names as Hen of the Woods, chanterelles, and black trumpets all have a woodsy flavor, reminiscent of the fall harvest. To me they are a special treat, harvested by hand by foragers twice a year. When I have them, I try to make them the star of the show. Paired with creamy polenta, stone-ground grits, or even pasta, this ragout really shines.

2 tablespoons olive oil

3 tablespoons unsalted butter

¾ cup diced onions

1 tablespoon minced garlic

2 pounds wild mushrooms, cleaned, stemmed, and quartered

2 teaspoons chopped fresh thyme leaves

2 teaspoons chopped fresh oregano leaves

1 cup canned petite diced tomatoes, with juices

1 tablespoon tomato paste

2 cups mushroom, chicken, or veal stock, or canned low-sodium chicken broth

1¼ teaspoons kosher salt

¼ teaspoon freshly ground black pepper

1 tablespoon chopped fresh parsley leaves

Creamy Polenta (recipe follows)

½ cup grated Parmigiano-Reggiano cheese

2 tablespoons finely chopped fresh chives

1. Place a 12-inch skillet over medium-high heat, and add the olive oil and the butter. When the butter begins to foam, add the diced onions and sauté until translucent, 3 to 4 minutes. Add the garlic and cook until fragrant, about 30 seconds. Add the mushrooms and cook, stirring often, until they have released most of their liquid, about 10 minutes.

2. Add the thyme, oregano, diced tomatoes, tomato paste, and stock, and bring to a boil. Reduce the heat to a simmer and cook, stirring occasionally, until the liquid has reduced and the ragout has thickened, about 20 minutes. Season with the salt and pepper, and stir in the parsley.

3. Divide the Creamy Polenta among four to six shallow bowls, and top with the mushroom ragout. Garnish with the Parmesan and chives, and serve hot.

4 to 6 servings

CREAMY POLENTA

Polenta, a northern Italian staple, is a dish made from ground cornmeal that is cooked into a porridge-like consistency. Polenta is always in my pantry at home—I love that it has so many uses. When I have leftover cooked polenta, I spread it out on a pan to cool in the fridge; the next day, I cut it into squares and fry it up. Served with a little homemade tomato sauce and some grated Parmesan cheese, it makes for a nice lunch.

4 cups whole milk

2 cups chicken stock or canned low-sodium chicken broth

4 tablespoons (½ stick) butter

2 teaspoons salt

¼ teaspoon freshly ground white pepper

⅛ teaspoon ground mace

1¾ cups stone-ground polenta (coarse cornmeal)

1 cup grated Parmigiano-Reggiano cheese

½ cup mascarpone or cream cheese

1. Combine the milk, chicken stock, butter, salt, white pepper, and mace in a large saucepan, and bring to a boil over high heat. Whisk in the polenta and stir continuously until the mixture begins to thicken. Then reduce the heat to medium-low and cook, stirring frequently, for 30 minutes, or until the polenta is creamy and tender.

2. Add the Parmesan and the mascarpone, and stir to blend. Remove from the heat and stir for 3 minutes to cool the polenta.

3. Serve immediately or keep warm until ready to use. (Leftover polenta is easily reheated in a small saucepan with a little water or milk to soften it.)

4 to 6 servings

SMOTHERED SHRIMP AND ANDOUILLE OVER STONE-GROUND GRITS

When the shrimper gets your shrimp for ya, use it all. There's nothing like it. Included here is a recipe for shrimp stock so that every morsel of shrimp goodness can be enjoyed.

. . . .

1 tablespoon olive oil

2 tablespoons butter

3 pounds large (21–25 count) head-on shrimp, peeled and deveined (heads and shells reserved for making stock)

1 tablespoon sweet paprika

1½ teaspoons salt

¼ teaspoon cayenne pepper

6 ounces andouille or other smoked sausage, cut into small dice (about 1 cup)

1 cup diced onions (small dice)

1 tablespoon minced garlic

2 tablespoons minced shallot

1 tablespoon minced green onion bottoms (white part)

2 cups chopped vine-ripened tomatoes

1 cup Shrimp Stock (recipe follows), chicken stock, or vegetable stock

⅓ cup sour cream

2 tablespoons minced green onion tops (green part)

Creamy Stone-Ground Grits (page 223)

2 tablespoons chopped fresh parsley leaves

1. Place a 12-inch sauté pan over medium-high heat, and add the olive oil. Once the oil is hot, add 1 tablespoon of the butter to the pan. While the butter is melting, season the shrimp with the paprika, salt, and cayenne. Add the shrimp to the pan and sear them for 1½ minutes per side. Transfer the shrimp to a plate, and set it aside.

2. Add the remaining 1 tablespoon butter to the sauté pan, and when it has melted, add the andouille. Cook, stirring often, until most of the fat has rendered and the andouille is crispy, 3 minutes. Add the onions and sauté for 2 minutes, stirring often. Add the garlic, shallot, and green onion bottoms, and cook for 1 minute. Add the tomatoes and cook for 1 minute. Raise the heat to high, add the shrimp stock, and cook, stirring occasionally, until most of the liquid has evaporated, about 5 minutes. Add the sour cream and stir to combine.

3. Return the shrimp to the sauté pan and fold them into the sauce. Cook until the shrimp are cooked through and hot, about 3 minutes. Stir in the green onion tops. Spoon the shrimp and sauce over the hot grits, garnish with the parsley, and serve while hot.

4 entrée servings, 6 appetizer servings

SHRIMP STOCK

This is an easy way to discover the virtues of homemade stock, if you've never made a fresh stock before. You don't need a huge pot, and you only have shells from 3 pounds of shrimp. This will allow you to experience the deepest, sweetest, delicate essence of shrimp. You will never throw another shrimp shell away.

1 to 1½ pounds shrimp shells and heads

1 cup roughly chopped onions

½ cup roughly chopped celery

½ cup roughly chopped carrots

2 cloves garlic, smashed with the side of a heavy knife

2 bay leaves

1 teaspoon salt

2 teaspoons black peppercorns

3 sprigs fresh thyme

1. Rinse the shrimp shells and heads in a large colander under cold running water.

2. Put all of the ingredients in a heavy-bottomed stockpot, and add enough water to cover by 1 inch (about 3½ quarts). Bring to a boil over high heat, skimming off the foam that forms on the surface. Reduce the heat to medium-low, and simmer for 45 minutes to 1 hour.

3. Strain the stock through a fine-mesh sieve into a large container. Let it cool completely; then cover and refrigerate. (The stock can be refrigerated for up to 3 days, or frozen in airtight containers for up to 2 months.)

About 3 quarts

CREAMY STONE-GROUND GRITS

Authentic grits, full of corn flavor, are ground between stones the old-fashioned way to leave bits and pieces of the outer germ layer intact. The simple truth is that true stone-ground grits taste nothing like the run-of-the-mill kind you find on most supermarket shelves. South Carolina is famous for 'em. They take longer to cook, but they're well worth the wait.

3 cups water

3 cups whole milk

1 teaspoon salt

½ teaspoon freshly ground white pepper

2 tablespoons butter

¾ cup stone-ground grits

8 ounces white cheddar cheese, grated (about 2 cups)

1. Combine the water, milk, salt, pepper, and 1 tablespoon of the butter in a medium saucepan, and bring to a boil over medium heat. Whisk in the grits. Cook, stirring frequently, for 1¼ to 1½ hours. Grits are ready when they are creamy and tender throughout. (It is important to stir often so that the grits do not stick to the bottom of the pan. If the grits absorb all of the water and milk before they are done, add hot water as needed to thin them out until they reach the desired consistency.)

2. Remove the pan from the heat and stir in the remaining 1 tablespoon butter and the cheese. Serve immediately. (The grits can be prepared in advance and reheated over very low heat.)

4 servings

GUMBO Z'HERBES WITH SMOKED HAM AND WILD RICE

Gumbo z'herbes is popular in New Orleans during the Lenten season because this hearty green stew usually does not include meat or stock. I love that dish, but I wanted to make it a little more dynamic, so I added ham to give it a smoky flavor, and instead of using white rice I use wild rice. With its nutty flavor and chewy texture, the wild rice really makes this gumbo z'herbes extraordinary.

1½ tablespoons olive oil or vegetable oil

1 small onion, chopped

3 tablespoons chopped green onions, white and light green parts, plus more for garnish

½ tablespoon chopped garlic

8 ounces smoked ham, diced

8 ounces fresh spinach, tough stems removed, leaves rinsed and coarsely chopped

8 ounces fresh collard greens, tough stems removed, leaves rinsed and coarsely chopped

8 ounces fresh turnip greens, tough stems removed, leaves rinsed and coarsely chopped

8 ounces cabbage, cored and coarsely chopped

3 quarts chicken stock or canned low-sodium chicken broth

1 cup wild rice

2 or 3 small bay leaves

1 teaspoon salt, plus more if needed

Cayenne pepper, to taste

Pinch of ground thyme

1 tablespoon filé powder, or more to taste (optional)

Chopped fresh parsley leaves, for garnish

1. Heat the oil in a large soup pot. Add the onion, green onions, and garlic, and cook until tender, about 3 minutes. Add the ham and cook for 2 minutes. A handful at a time, add the spinach, collards, turnip greens, and cabbage, stirring them until wilted before adding the next bunch. Then add the stock, wild rice, bay leaves, salt, cayenne, and thyme. Bring to a boil. Reduce the heat to a simmer and cook for 1 hour.

2. Taste, and adjust the seasoning if needed—the greens should be tender and slightly spicy. The wild rice should be tender and puffed.

3. If you wish to thicken it, stir 1 tablespoon filé powder into the simmering gumbo. Add more filé, a little at a time, until thickened. Simmer for 3 minutes more. (Do not allow the gumbo to boil once you have added the filé.)

4. Serve garnished with chopped parsley and green onions.

6 to 8 servings

MARINATED BLUE CRAB CLAWS

Save the claws the next time you have a crab boil at your house, or purchase them already peeled from a local seafood market. However you go about getting your crab claws, this simple, toss-together dish makes for a festive party hors d'oeuvre. Make it a day or two ahead of time and pull it out of the fridge just in time for the party. Now *that's* what I'm talking about!

½ cup extra-virgin olive oil

2 tablespoons red wine vinegar

1 tablespoon freshly squeezed
  lemon juice

¼ cup chopped green onions, white
  and green parts

2 tablespoons minced shallot

2 tablespoons minced celery

2 tablespoons chopped fresh
  parsley leaves

1 tablespoon chopped fresh basil
  leaves

2 teaspoons minced garlic

2 teaspoons Worcestershire sauce

1 teaspoon chopped fresh oregano
  leaves

¼ cup thinly sliced pimento-stuffed
  green olives

1 teaspoon salt

½ teaspoon freshly ground black
  pepper

½ teaspoon hot pepper sauce

1 pound cooked blue crab claws,
  outer shells removed

1. Combine all the ingredients except the crab claws in a large nonreactive bowl, and whisk to mix well. Add the crab claws and toss to coat. Cover, and refrigerate for at least 6 hours or as long as overnight.

2. Serve chilled or at cool room temperature in individual serving bowls or allow guests to serve themselves from a large bowl.

6 to 8 appetizer servings

SMOKED TROUT "SOUFFLÉ"

This is a cold soufflé—really more of a mousse that is set with gelatin, resembling a hot soufflé in appearance only. I love to serve this at cocktail parties, with crisp toasts or crackers for dipping. This creamy concoction tastes delightfully light and is sure to make a big splash.

2 cups cold heavy cream

2 packets unflavored powdered gelatin

1 pound smoked trout, skin removed and discarded, flesh flaked

2 tablespoons minced shallot

2 tablespoons chopped fresh parsley leaves

1 tablespoon minced chives

1 teaspoon freshly ground white pepper

1. Pour 1 cup of the heavy cream into a medium bowl. Sprinkle the gelatin over the cream, and stir to incorporate. Let it sit for 5 minutes to soften.

2. Meanwhile, pour the remaining 1 cup cream into a saucepan and bring it to a boil.

3. Pour the hot cream over the cold cream, and whisk to combine.

4. Combine the trout, shallot, parsley, chives, and pepper in the bowl of a food processor, and process until smooth, about 20 seconds. While the machine is running, gradually add the cream mixture, processing until well combined.

5. Cut a piece of parchment paper to measure 4 × 12 inches. Wrap the parchment around the outside of a 12-ounce ramekin to form an upright collar, and tape it in place. Spoon the mousse into the ramekin, smooth the top with a spatula, and wrap it in plastic wrap. Refrigerate for at least 4 hours, and up to 24.

6. Serve the "soufflé" with toast points, croutons, or crackers.

8 to 10 hors d'oeuvre servings

MARYLAND CRAB TOAST

Make sure you use the freshest crabmeat available for this simple treat. And, hey, even if you buy it already picked, take the time to go through the crabmeat again to make sure there aren't any remaining bits of shell or cartilage.

12 slices ciabatta, sourdough, or other artisanal bread

1 pint fresh lump crabmeat

½ cup finely chopped celery

¼ cup finely chopped fresh chives

2 tablespoons whole-grain mustard

2 tablespoons mayonnaise, store-bought or homemade (see page 153)

Juice of 1 lemon

Salt and freshly ground black pepper, to taste

18 ounces Gruyère cheese, sliced

1. Preheat the oven to 350°F.

2. Arrange the bread in a single layer on a baking sheet, and set it aside.

3. In a medium bowl, combine the crabmeat, celery, chives, mustard, mayonnaise, and lemon juice. Season with salt and pepper to taste, and mix well. Spread approximately 3 tablespoons of the crabmeat mixture evenly over each piece of bread. Arrange the sliced Gruyère over the crabmeat mixture. Bake until the cheese has melted, about 10 minutes. Serve immediately.

12 servings

NEW ENGLAND LOBSTER ROLLS

There's nothing like going directly to the dock to pick up fresh lobsters. All along the New England coast, there are clam shacks and seafood joints that specialize in fresh clams, lobsters, and fish. Most of these places serve lobster rolls. Nothing fancy: just fresh lobster, a little mayo, and some herbs, all served on a soft hot dog bun. Got to love it!

4 hot dog buns

4 tablespoons (½ stick) unsalted butter, melted

⅓ cup mayonnaise, homemade (see page 153) or good-quality store-bought

2 teaspoons freshly squeezed lemon juice

½ teaspoon salt

¼ cup finely chopped celery

1 tablespoon minced shallot

1 tablespoon minced fresh tarragon leaves

1 tablespoon minced fresh parsley leaves

1 teaspoon chopped fresh chives

1 pound freshly cooked lobster tail and claw meat, cubed (from two 1¾-pound lobsters)

Potato chips, for serving

1. Preheat the grill or broiler.

2. Using a pastry brush, spread the inside and outside of each bun with the melted butter. Grill or broil the buns quickly to warm them through. Set the buns aside.

3. Combine the mayonnaise, lemon juice, and salt in a bowl, and mix well. Fold in the celery, shallot, tarragon, parsley, and chives. Then fold in the lobster meat. Place 1 bun on each plate, and divide the lobster salad evenly among the buns.

4. Serve immediately, with potato chips alongside.

4 servings

SPANISH-STYLE BRAISED SQUID

To me squid is an underrated ingredient. It really lends itself to just about any flavoring and cooking method. Whether it is grilled, sautéed, fried, or braised, it can be sweet, tender, and truly delicious. I love to serve this dish as a part of a small plate menu.

. . . .

¼ cup olive oil

¾ cup sliced onions

3 tablespoons sliced garlic

½ cup dry white wine, such as Albariño

1 pound squid, tentacles removed and reserved, bodies cut into thin rings

3 teaspoons chopped fresh parsley leaves

1½ teaspoons chopped fresh oregano leaves

1½ teaspoons freshly squeezed lemon juice

1 teaspoon nonpareil capers, drained

¾ teaspoon salt

Generous ¼ teaspoon freshly ground black pepper

¼ teaspoon hot pimentón (smoked Spanish paprika)

Warm crusty bread, for serving

1. Combine the olive oil and onions in a large sauté pan over medium heat, and cook until the onions are beginning to caramelize, 3 to 4 minutes. Then add the garlic and cook for 2 minutes longer. Add the white wine and reduce for 2 minutes. Add the squid (tentacles and rings), parsley, oregano, lemon juice, capers, salt, pepper, and pimentón. Cook until the squid is tender, 5 to 6 minutes.

2. Serve with the crusty bread.

4 to 6 tapas-size servings

SIMPLE OYSTER "STEW"

Though Louisiana folks refer to this creamy soup as a stew, don't let the name fool you. This simple, brothy delicacy is the perfect way to showcase plump, salty oysters. Use the best quality milk and butter you can find, and make sure you stir in any oyster liquor that arrives with the shucked oysters. Serve with oyster crackers or hot crusty bread, and you're there!

5 tablespoons unsalted butter

¼ cup finely chopped celery

3 tablespoons all-purpose flour

5 cups whole milk

1 cup heavy cream

¾ teaspoon salt, plus more if needed

½ teaspoon freshly ground white pepper

½ teaspoon cayenne pepper

½ cup finely sliced green onions (green tops only)

1 garlic clove, smashed

2 pints shucked oysters, with any oyster liquor

4 ounces fresh baby spinach leaves, rinsed and spun dry (optional)

1. Melt 2 tablespoons of the butter in a large soup pot over medium-low heat, and add the celery. Cook, stirring occasionally, until the celery is very soft, about 4 minutes. Stir in the flour and cook, stirring, for 2 minutes; do not allow the flour to brown. Working quickly, whisk in the milk and cream, and raise the heat to medium. Continue to cook, stirring frequently, until the liquid thickens a bit and comes to a gentle simmer. Add ½ teaspoon of the salt and the white pepper, cayenne, green onions, and garlic clove. Continue to cook until the soup thickens a bit more and the flavors come together, 5 to 10 minutes.

2. Remove and discard the smashed garlic clove. Stir in the oysters, along with any oyster liquor, and cook, stirring frequently, until the edges of the oysters are beginning to curl, 4 to 5 minutes. Stir in the spinach, if using, and cook until it has wilted and the oysters are just cooked through, 2 to 3 minutes. Taste, and add the remaining ¼ teaspoon salt (or more if needed). Serve immediately in wide shallow bowls, each bowl garnished with ½ tablespoon of the remaining butter.

2¹/₂ quarts, 6 servings

DILL AND BLACK PEPPER GRAVLAX WITH MINI POTATO PANCAKES AND CHIVE SOUR CREAM

Preserve this ocean treasure by burying it in herbs and spices. Take a beautiful side of wild salmon, cure it for a day and a half, slice it thin, and indulge. This is an intensely flavored dish that melts in your mouth. Are you ready? Serve it with potato cakes and chive sour cream to enrich the experience.

½ cup kosher salt

½ cup sugar

¼ cup coarsely cracked black pepper

One 3-pound side of wild salmon, such as coho or king, scaled, pinbones removed

¼ cup chopped fresh dill

Mini Potato Pancakes (recipe follows), for serving

Chive Sour Cream (recipe follows), for serving

1. Combine the salt, sugar, and cracked black pepper in a mixing bowl. Transfer half the mixture to a non-reactive pan or baking dish that is large enough to hold the salmon. (If you don't have a large enough baking dish, line a rimmed baking sheet with enough plastic wrap to wrap around the salmon twice, and place half the mixture on the plastic wrap.)

2. Place the salmon, skin side down, on the salt mixture. Cover the flesh side of the salmon with the remaining salt mixture, rubbing it onto the salmon to distribute it evenly. Scatter the fresh dill on top, patting it down, and cover the salmon with plastic wrap. Place a flat-bottomed container the size of the salmon (such as another baking dish or baking sheet) on top of the salmon, and weight it with a heavy object such as an iron skillet, bricks, or a few cans. Refrigerate the salmon for 24 hours, flipping it occasionally to ensure even curing and redistributing the cure as necessary. As the salmon cures, its moisture is drawn out to produce a brine. Remove the plastic and check the salmon for firmness. If it still feels fleshy, lay it flesh side down directly in the brine. Continue to cure for up to 12 hours, or until the thickest part of the salmon is firm.

3. Remove the salmon from the refrigerator and pat it dry. Set it, skin side down, on a wire rack set over a baking sheet, and allow it to air-dry in the refrigerator for an hour or two. (The cured salmon can be wrapped tightly in plastic wrap or parchment paper and stored in the refrigerator for up to 2 weeks.)

4. Slice the salmon as thin as possible with a very sharp knife, and serve with the Mini Potato Pancakes and Chive Sour Cream. Alternatively, sliced salmon may be diced (skin removed beforehand) and served with traditional garnishes tartare-fashion (boiled eggs, red onion, capers, toast points, and an herb oil, pages 2–3).

6 to 8 servings

MINI POTATO PANCAKES

These delights are incredibly delicious on their own. Serve them for breakfast or as a side dish. Just please don't let the kids add ketchup! Unless, of course, you made it yourself.

. . . .

2 pounds Idaho potatoes

½ cup minced onion

2 eggs, lightly beaten

2 tablespoons all-purpose flour

¼ teaspoon baking powder

1 teaspoon kosher salt

½ teaspoon freshly ground black pepper

Vegetable oil for frying

1. Peel the potatoes, and grate them on the large holes of a box grater or using the large grate disc on a food processor. Using a kitchen towel, wring the grated potatoes dry in two batches. Add the potatoes and onion to a mixing bowl, and toss gently with the eggs. Add the flour, baking powder, salt, and pepper, and mix well.

2. Pour enough vegetable oil into a large skillet to reach a depth of ⅛ inch, and heat it over medium-high heat. When the oil is hot, add the pancake mixture by tablespoonfuls. Gently flatten each pancake with the back of a fork, and pan-fry until golden brown, about 2 to 3 minutes on each side. Remove from the oil and drain on paper towels. Repeat with the remaining pancake mixture, adding more oil as needed between batches.

36 potato pancakes

CHIVE SOUR CREAM

1 cup sour cream

¼ cup minced fresh chives

1 teaspoon kosher salt

½ teaspoon freshly ground black pepper

Combine all the ingredients in a small bowl. Cover and refrigerate until ready to use, up to 1 week.

1 cup

BAKED GULF OYSTERS AND SHRIMP WITH GARLIC, LEMON BUTTER, AND CRABMEAT

This dish is one of the biggest sellers at my restaurant in Gulfport, Mississippi. We benefit from the bounty of incredible fresh seafood that comes in from the Gulf waters. It doesn't get much better than this.

8 tablespoons (1 stick) unsalted butter, at room temperature

2 tablespoons minced garlic

1 tablespoon minced shallot

1 tablespoon minced fresh parsley leaves, plus more for garnish

¾ teaspoon salt

¼ teaspoon freshly ground white pepper

1 pint shucked raw oysters, drained well and patted dry on paper towels

8 ounces medium shrimp, peeled and deveined

4 ounces fresh crabmeat, picked over for shells and cartilage

⅓ cup fine dry unseasoned breadcrumbs

⅓ cup finely grated Parmigiano-Reggiano cheese

1 tablespoon olive oil

Lemon wedges, for serving

1. In a small bowl, combine the butter, garlic, shallot, parsley, salt, and pepper. Refrigerate for 10 minutes.

2. Position an oven rack in the upper third of the oven, and preheat the broiler.

3. Divide the oysters and shrimp among eight individual gratin dishes just large enough to hold the oysters in one layer, such as 8-ounce shallow gratin dishes. Sprinkle the crabmeat evenly over the oysters and shrimp. Divide the compound butter evenly among the ramekins. Transfer the dishes to a large baking sheet, and broil for about 5 minutes, or until the oysters and shrimp are beginning to firm up.

4. While the ramekins are broiling, combine the breadcrumbs, 3 tablespoons of the Parmesan, and the olive oil in a bowl. Stir to blend.

5. Remove the ramekins from the broiler, and sprinkle the crumb mixture evenly over the seafood. Return the ramekins to the broiler and broil until the crumbs are golden brown and the oysters and shrimp are just cooked through and curled around the edges, 3 to 4 minutes.

6. Remove the ramekins from the oven, garnish with the remaining Parmesan, and serve immediately, with lemon wedges alongside.

8 appetizer servings

LITTLENECK CLAMS WITH SWEET ITALIAN SAUSAGE AND SPICY TOMATO SAUCE

Oh, baby, this simple clam and pasta dish will have you coming back for more. Feel free to use spicy Italian sausage in place of the mild, if you prefer.

8 ounces linguine or spaghettini

2 tablespoons olive oil, plus more for drizzling

1 pound fresh sweet Italian sausage, removed from casings and crumbled

½ cup finely chopped yellow onion

3 tablespoons thinly sliced garlic

2 teaspoons chopped fresh oregano leaves

½ teaspoon salt

¼ teaspoon crushed red pepper

½ cup dry white wine

½ cup bottled clam juice

1 can (14.5 ounces) petite diced tomatoes, with their liquid

2 pounds littleneck clams, scrubbed and purged in water (see Note)

2 teaspoons freshly squeezed lemon juice

1 tablespoon extra-virgin olive oil

3 tablespoons finely chopped fresh parsley leaves

½ cup finely grated Parmigiano-Reggiano cheese, or to taste

1. Bring a large pot of salted water to a boil. Add the linguine and cook until al dente according to package directions, about 8 minutes. Drain the pasta in a colander, and lightly drizzle it with olive oil. Toss well to coat, and set aside.

2. Heat the 2 tablespoons olive oil in a large, heavy sauté pan or medium pot over medium-high heat. Add the sausage and cook, stirring occasionally, until the sausage is lightly browned, 2 to 3 minutes. Add the onion and cook, stirring, until soft, 3 to 4 minutes. Add the garlic, oregano, salt, and crushed red pepper and cook, stirring, for about 1 minute. Add the wine, clam juice, and tomatoes. Stir to mix well, and simmer until the sauce has reduced a bit and thickened slightly, about 10 minutes.

3. Add the clams, cover the pan, and cook, shaking the pan occasionally, until the clams open, about 5 minutes. Discard any unopened clams.

4. Stir in the lemon juice and the cooked pasta. Cook, tossing frequently, until the pasta is heated through, about 1 minute. Add the extra-virgin olive oil and parsley, and toss to coat well. Divide among serving bowls and top with the Parmesan cheese. Serve immediately.

Note: Clams live buried in the sandy bottom of the ocean floor. They accumulate grit, sand, and dirt because they do not fully close their shells. Live clams need to be purged of the sand and grit prior to cooking. In order to purge clams, they must be submerged in a saltwater solution of ⅓ cup salt mixed with 1 gallon of water. The clams should sit in the solution for 30 minutes. At this time the water should be changed to ensure that there is enough oxygen so the clams do not suffocate. This process should be repeated 2 or 3 times. Alternatively, the clams can be left in a large amount of water overnight.

4 servings

SAUTÉED SOFT-SHELL CRABS

Soft-shell crab season starts around mid-April on the Gulf Coast, all the way from Texas to Florida. The season lasts longer here than anywhere else because the waters of the Gulf of Mexico stay nice and warm all the way into the month of October. Soft-shell crabs are a delicacy because of their sweet, briny flavor and their delicate soft shells, which allow us to eat the whole thing.

4 soft-shell crabs, cleaned (see Note)

1 teaspoon salt

½ teaspoon freshly ground white pepper

1 cup Wondra flour

3 tablespoons olive oil

2 tablespoons butter

1 tablespoon chopped shallot

1 tablespoon chopped fresh parsley leaves

1 teaspoon minced garlic

1. Preheat the oven to 400°F.

2. Season the crabs with the salt and pepper. Place the flour in a shallow dish and dredge the crabs in it, shaking off any excess.

3. Heat the olive oil in a large heavy ovenproof skillet over moderately high heat until it is hot but not smoking. Carefully place the crabs in the skillet, top shell down (they may sputter and pop). Cook the crabs until they begin to blister, about 3 minutes. Flip them over and immediately transfer the skillet to the oven. Bake for 2 to 3 minutes.

4. Remove the skillet from the oven and transfer the crabs to serving plates or a platter. Add the butter, shallot, parsley, and garlic to the hot skillet and cook over medium-low heat for 2 minutes, or until the butter begins to turn brown.

5. Serve the crabs drizzled with the brown butter.

Note: To clean soft-shell crabs, rinse them under cold running water and brush them with a small brush to remove any dirt from their outer shells, if necessary. Twist off and discard the apron. Fold back the pointed sides of the top shell to expose the gills; remove the gills on both sides. Using kitchen scissors, cut across the front of the crab, about ¼ inch behind the eyes and mouth, and squeeze out the small sac hiding directly behind the mouth. The crabs are now ready to be cooked.

2 entrée servings, 4 appetizer servings

SAUTÉED REDFISH WITH PECAN-SHALLOT COMPOUND BUTTER

There was a time when Louisiana redfish were fished to near depletion, but thanks to strict regulations they have made a strong comeback and are thriving and plentiful in Gulf waters. This is one of the tastiest and certainly one of the most popular fish along the Gulf Coast. Redfish and pecans is a classic Louisiana pairing, and topped with fresh Louisiana crabmeat, this dish is a knockout.

2 tablespoons olive oil

1½ teaspoons salt

¾ teaspoon freshly ground white pepper

Four 6-ounce redfish fillets, scaled, skin scored, or another firm-fleshed fish, such as striped bass or red snapper

8 tablespoons (1 stick) unsalted butter, at room temperature, cut into pieces

4 teaspoons minced shallot

½ cup chopped pecans

8 ounces fresh lump crabmeat, picked over for shells and cartilage

3 tablespoons freshly squeezed lemon juice

4 pats Pecan-Shallot Compound Butter (recipe follows)

1 teaspoon chopped fresh parsley leaves

1 teaspoon chopped fresh chives

1 teaspoon chopped fresh tarragon leaves

1. Preheat the oven to 450°F.

2. Set a 14-inch ovenproof sauté pan over high heat and add the olive oil.

3. While the oil is heating, season the fish fillets on both sides with 1 teaspoon of the salt and ½ teaspoon of the white pepper.

4. When the oil is very hot, add the fillets, skin side down, and cook until crisp around the edges, about 1 minute. Turn the fillets over, and add the butter, shallot, and pecans to the pan. Transfer the pan to the oven and bake until the butter is beginning to brown around the edges and the fish is almost cooked through, about 5 minutes.

5. Remove the pan from the oven and add the crabmeat. Drizzle the lemon juice over the butter, and return the pan to the oven. Bake for 2 minutes, or until the fish is just cooked through.

6. Remove the pan from the oven, place 1 pat of the compound butter on each piece of fish, and set each piece on a serving plate.

7. Season the pecans and crabmeat in the pan with the remaining ½ teaspoon salt and remaining ¼ teaspoon pepper. Add the parsley, chives, and tarragon, and stir to combine. Then spoon the pecan-crabmeat relish evenly over the fillets, and serve immediately.

4 servings

PECAN-SHALLOT COMPOUND BUTTER

I'm going to tell you right now: you'll wish you made more of this. Go ahead, double the recipe! Whatever you don't use on the fish can be frozen and whipped out at a moment's notice. Toss it with pasta or steamed vegetables, or smear it over pan-roasted chicken.

¼ cup pecan pieces

4 tablespoons (½ stick) unsalted butter, cut into pieces, at room temperature

½ tablespoon minced shallot

½ teaspoon chopped garlic

¼ teaspoon salt

1. Preheat the oven to 400°F. Cut out a 5-inch square of parchment paper, and set it aside.

2. Spread the pecans on a baking sheet, and bake them in the oven until lightly toasted, 7 to 10 minutes. Remove from the oven and let cool. Roughly chop.

3. Place the cooled pecans in a small bowl. Add the butter, shallot, garlic, and salt, and mix well with a rubber spatula. Spoon the mixture down the middle of the parchment paper, and roll it into a log, about 1 inch in diameter. Wrap tightly and refrigerate until ready to use, up to 1 week. (The butter can be frozen, tightly wrapped in plastic, for up to 1 month.)

⅓ **cup**

PAN-ROASTED STRIPED BASS WITH FAVA BEAN–CHORIZO RAGOUT

Sautéed fresh fish, sausage, and fava beans in a creamy broth: you will enjoy every morsel. Use a spoon to get every drop.

2 cups shelled fresh fava beans

4 tablespoons olive oil

8 ounces smoked chorizo, cut into ¼-inch-thick half-moons

8 ounces bulk fresh chorizo, crumbled

1 cup diced onions (small dice)

1 cup chicken stock or canned low-sodium chicken broth

1½ teaspoons salt

¼ cup heavy cream

1 tablespoon chopped fresh thyme leaves

1 tablespoon chopped fresh parsley leaves

1 teaspoon chopped fresh oregano leaves

1 teaspoon cayenne pepper

Four 8-ounce striped bass fillets, skin on

1. Place a large pot of water over high heat. Add enough salt so that the water tastes salty, and bring to a rapid boil.

2. While the water heats, prepare an ice bath. Set the bowl aside.

3. Add the fava beans to the boiling water in batches, to ensure that the water doesn't lose its boil. Cook for 3 to 5 minutes, depending on the size of the fava beans, until the beans are crisp-tender or al dente; larger beans will cook in closer to 5 minutes. Using a large slotted spoon or a strainer, quickly remove the beans from the boiling water and submerge them in the ice bath. As soon as they are no longer warm, remove them from the ice bath. Remove the thin skin covering the beans and set the beans aside.

4. Heat 2 tablespoons of the olive oil in a large sauté pan over medium-high heat. When it is hot, add the smoked chorizo, fresh chorizo, and onions. Cook until the onions begin to soften and the sausage starts to caramelize, about 4 minutes. (If necessary, use the back of a spoon to break the fresh sausage into smaller pieces, roughly the same size as the fava beans.)

5. Add the fava beans and the stock, and bring to a boil. Then reduce the heat, cover the pan, and simmer for 6 to 8 minutes until tender. Season with ½ teaspoon of the salt. Add the heavy cream and continue to cook, uncovered, until the sauce has thickened slightly, about 3 minutes. Stir in the thyme, parsley, and oregano, remove from the heat, and keep warm.

6. Season the striped bass fillets on both sides with the remaining 1 teaspoon salt and the cayenne pepper.

7. Place a large sauté pan over medium-high heat, and when it is hot, add the remaining 2 tablespoons olive oil. Place the fillets, skin side down, in the pan, and cook for 4 minutes. If the fillets begin to curl, press them down gently with a spatula. Turn the fillets over and cook for another 2 minutes.

8. Divide the fava bean–chorizo ragout among four plates, and top each one with a fish fillet. Serve immediately.

4 servings

SEARED DIVER SCALLOPS WITH ORANGES, OLIVES, CAPERS, AND FENNEL PUREE

You may ask, "What is the difference between a diver scallop and a regular scallop?" Diver scallops are harvested by hand, whereas regular scallops are farmed or collected in nets that sweep the ocean floor. Because diver scallops are collected by hand, only the largest scallops are taken, generally leaving the smaller ones behind to continue to grow. The scallops are brought to market almost immediately—meaning they are at their absolute best.

16 large (U-10) diver scallops

1½ teaspoons salt

1 teaspoon freshly ground white pepper

2 tablespoons olive oil

½ cup freshly squeezed orange juice

¼ cup dry white wine

4 tablespoons (½ stick) butter, cut into small cubes

1 cup orange segments (from about 2 oranges)

⅓ cup pitted and sliced Cerignola olives

1 tablespoon nonpareil capers, drained

1 tablespoon chopped fresh parsley leaves

Fennel Puree (recipe follows)

1. Preheat the oven to 400°F.

2. Season the scallops on both sides with 1 teaspoon of the salt and ½ teaspoon of the white pepper.

3. Place a large sauté pan over high heat. When it is hot, add the olive oil and half of the scallops. Cook the scallops on one side for 1 minute, until they are golden brown. Turn the scallops over and cook on the second side for 1 minute. Transfer the scallops to an ovenproof platter, and repeat with the remaining scallops. Then place the scallops in the oven and bake until they are just cooked through, 4 to 5 minutes.

4. Meanwhile, discard the olive oil remaining in the sauté pan. Add the orange juice and the white wine to the hot pan, and cook over medium-high heat for 2 minutes, or until reduced to a syrupy consistency. Add a few cubes of butter, swirling the pan or whisking the butter in to form an emulsion. Then add the remaining butter in increments, allowing each addition to be fully incorporated before adding more. Season the sauce with the remaining ½ teaspoon salt and ½ teaspoon pepper. Add the orange segments, olives, and capers, and simmer until just warmed through. Do not allow the sauce to boil.

5. Remove the scallops from the oven. Divide the warm Fennel Puree between each of four plates. Place 4 scallops on top of the fennel puree, and then spoon the sauce around each plate. Serve immediately.

4 servings

FENNEL PUREE

Fennel is a natural complement to seafood, and it is a wonderful backdrop for the scallops. This puree is simple to prepare and provides a clean, light, and slightly sweet anise flavor. Pair it with roasted potatoes and glazed carrots for a true study in contrasts.

3 tablespoons unsalted butter

1 tablespoon olive oil

2 fennel bulbs, cored and thinly sliced

¼ cup water

3 tablespoons crème fraîche, store-bought or homemade (see page 134)

½ teaspoon sea salt

½ teaspoon freshly ground white pepper

1. Combine the butter and the olive oil in a medium saucepan over medium-low heat. When the butter begins to bubble, add the fennel and stir to coat. Add the water, cover the pan, and cook for 20 to 22 minutes, stirring occasionally. The fennel will begin to release some of its juices and become translucent. Do not allow the fennel to brown; reduce the heat if it begins to brown before it is tender.

2. Transfer the fennel to a blender. Add the crème fraiche, salt, and pepper, and blend until smooth. Strain the puree through a fine-mesh sieve into a bowl, and discard any solids. Serve warm. (The puree can be made 1 day in advance and gently reheated.)

2 cups

out on the range

BACON-WRAPPED QUAIL WITH SAUSAGE, SAGE, AND CHESTNUT DRESSING

Quail have always been a favorite of chefs for their delicate meat and robust flavor, and they are now gaining popularity with home cooks as they become more available from small farms around the country. The key to cooking quail is to cook it at a high heat for a short period of time. Wrapping quail in bacon not only adds flavor but also guarantees that these little birds stay moist.

8 strips bacon

4 tablespoons (½ stick) unsalted butter

2 celery stalks, cut into small dice

1 medium onion, cut into small dice

Salt and freshly ground black pepper

12 ounces sweet fennel sausage or mild Italian sausage, casings removed

1½ tablespoons chiffonade of fresh sage leaves (see Note, page 86)

1½ teaspoons chopped fresh thyme leaves

8 ounces roasted chestnuts, peeled and roughly chopped (see Note, page 254)

3 cups crustless bread cubes (from a hearty bread such as peasant loaf or Italian), lightly toasted

¾ cup turkey or chicken stock, or canned low-sodium chicken broth, plus more as needed to soften the bread

2 tablespoons heavy cream

8 semi-boneless quail

About ¼ cup olive oil

1. Preheat the oven to 375°F. Butter a standard-size loaf pan, and set it aside. Line a small baking sheet with parchment paper.

2. Place the bacon strips on the parchment-lined baking sheet, and bake until some of the fat has been rendered and the bacon is lightly browned but still pliable, about 8 minutes. Remove from the baking sheet and set aside.

3. Melt 3 tablespoons of the butter in a medium skillet over medium heat. Add the celery and onion, and cook until the onion is almost translucent, 4 to 6 minutes. Season with a pinch of salt and pepper. Add the sausage and cook, stirring and breaking the sausage into small pieces with the spoon, until it is well browned, about 6 minutes. Stir in the sage, thyme, chestnuts, and bread cubes. Combine the stock and the heavy cream in a measuring cup, and season lightly with salt and pepper. Add the liquid, ¼ cup at a time, to the dressing mixture, stirring gently to combine until it is very moist. Arrange the stuffing in the prepared baking dish. Cut the remaining 1 tablespoon butter into small pieces and scatter them over the dressing. Bake until heated through, about 20 minutes. If the top gets too brown, cover with aluminum foil.

4. Remove the dressing from the oven and set it aside until cooled to room temperature.

5. Increase the oven temperature to 400°F.

6. Season the quail, inside and out, with salt and pepper. Spoon 3 tablespoons of the dressing into the cavity of each quail. Using a toothpick or a piece of kitchen twine, secure the legs together. Wrap 1 bacon strip around each quail, overlapping the ends and securing them with toothpicks. Place the quail on a rack on a rimmed baking dish. Brush the quail with a little olive oil, and roast in the oven for 15 to 18 minutes, until the birds are just cooked through and the juices run clear.

7. Remove the toothpicks and serve immediately.

Note: Chestnuts are a holiday favorite and can be found in two forms: raw in the shell or precooked and peeled in vacuum packed bags or in a jar. We prefer to use the jarred variety; a few of our favorite brands include Minerve, Sabaton, or Galil.

If you cannot find roasted chestnuts in your area, fresh, raw chestnuts can be roasted in the oven. Preheat the oven to 400°F. Using a sharp paring knife, cut an X in the round end of the chestnut. Spread the nuts on a rimmed baking sheet and sprinkle lightly with water. Roast in the oven for 10 minutes, stir the chestnuts well, and then continue to roast for 10 minutes longer. Carefully peel the chestnuts as soon as they are cool enough to handle. (Peel off both the outer shell and the inner shell.) Use immediately or store in the refrigerator in a resealable plastic container for up to 2 days.

4 entrée servings, 8 appetizer servings

ROAST CHICKEN WITH SORREL CREAM SAUCE

Sorrel is an herb with a tart, lemony flavor that pairs well with chicken and fish. If you cannot find sorrel in your local farmer's market or grocery store, by all means plant some in your garden. Sorrel grows wild like a weed and will flourish in your herb garden or even in containers in a sunny spot in your kitchen.

For the chicken

3 tablespoons butter, at room temperature

3 tablespoons finely chopped fresh sorrel leaves

One 4-pound chicken, cut into quarters

1 teaspoon salt

½ teaspoon freshly ground white pepper

1 lemon, quartered

1 cup chopped onions

2 cloves garlic

2 bay leaves

2 sprigs fresh lemon thyme

For the sauce

2 tablespoons butter

2 tablespoons minced shallot

½ cup dry white wine

1 cup heavy cream

1 tablespoon freshly squeezed lemon juice

1 cup very thinly sliced fresh sorrel leaves

1 cup slivered fresh spinach leaves

2 teaspoons chopped fresh tarragon leaves

½ teaspoon salt

¼ teaspoon freshly ground white pepper

1. Preheat the oven to 375°F.

2. Prepare the chicken: Combine the butter and sorrel in a small bowl. Rub the sorrel butter all over the chicken and under the skin. Season the chicken on both sides with the salt and pepper.

3. Place the chicken quarters in a roasting pan, and arrange the lemon quarters, chopped onions, garlic, bay leaves, and thyme sprigs around the chicken. Roast the chicken, uncovered, until it is cooked through and the juices run clear when pierced with a skewer, about 40 minutes. While the chicken is cooking, spoon the accumulated juices over the bird every 10 minutes or so to keep it moist.

4. Remove the chicken from the oven, and pour the pan juices into a small bowl. Cover the pan with aluminum foil, and set the chicken aside to rest for 15 minutes in a warm place.

5. While the chicken is resting, prepare the sauce: Melt the butter in a small saucepan, and add the shallot. Cook over low heat until the shallot is soft, 1½ to 2 minutes; do not allow it to brown. Add the wine and cook until it has reduced by one fourth. Add the heavy cream and cook for 3 minutes, until thickened. Add the lemon juice, sorrel, spinach, tarragon, and reserved pan juices, and cook until the greens are wilted, 2 to 3 minutes. Do not allow the sauce to boil. Season with the salt and pepper. Remove from the heat.

6. Transfer the roast chicken to serving plates, and spoon the sauce over all. Serve immediately.

4 servings

FRIED CHICKEN AND BUTTERMILK WAFFLES WITH BLACK PEPPER MAPLE SYRUP AND WHIPPED VANILLA BUTTER

This may seem an unlikely combination, but trust me, for those moments when you're not sure if it's dinner or breakfast that you want, this satisfies completely. Waffles stand in here in place of biscuits—and soak up all the buttery, syrupy goodness that is drizzled over the crisp-fried chicken. This recipe is based on a killer version of chicken and waffles that is served at Emeril's Restaurant in New Orleans.

1½ cups well-shaken buttermilk

¼ cup Crystal hot sauce or other Louisiana red hot sauce

1½ tablespoons sugar

1 tablespoon plus 1 teaspoon salt

1 tablespoon sweet paprika

3 cloves garlic, smashed

One 3½-pound chicken, cut into 8 pieces

2 cups all-purpose flour

3 to 4 cups vegetable oil, for frying

Buttermilk Waffles (recipe follows)

Black Pepper Maple Syrup (page 260)

Whipped Vanilla Butter (recipe follows)

1. In a small bowl, whisk together the buttermilk, hot sauce, sugar, the 1 tablespoon salt, and the paprika. Add the garlic. Transfer this mixture to a gallon-size resealable plastic food storage bag. Add the chicken pieces to the bag, seal, and refrigerate. Allow the chicken to marinate overnight, turning the bag occasionally to ensure that the chicken is evenly marinated.

2. Place a wire rack on a baking sheet, and set it aside. In a medium-size bowl, combine the flour with the remaining 1 teaspoon salt.

3. Remove the chicken pieces from the marinade, allowing the excess to drain off, and then dredge them in the flour. Set the coated pieces on the wire rack.

4. Pour oil to a depth of 1 inch in a 10-inch cast-iron skillet. Heat the oil over high heat to 350°F. (Use a deep-fry/candy thermometer for accuracy.)

5. Fry the chicken, in batches, until golden brown and cooked through, 6 to 8 minutes per side; the chicken should register 165°F on an instant-read thermometer. As you are cooking, be mindful of the temperature of your oil and regulate the heat as necessary. You do

not want the temperature of the oil to drop below 325°
or to go above 350°F. As the pieces are cooked, transfer them to a paper towel–lined platter.

6. Serve the chicken hot, with the Buttermilk Waffles, Black Pepper Maple Syrup, and Whipped Vanilla Butter.

4 to 6 servings

BUTTERMILK WAFFLES

1¾ cups cake flour

3 tablespoons sugar

2 tablespoons yellow cornmeal

½ teaspoon baking soda

½ teaspoon salt

2 cups well-shaken buttermilk

2 eggs

½ teaspoon vanilla extract

8 tablespoons (1 stick) butter, melted

1. Combine the flour, sugar, cornmeal, baking soda, and salt in a medium mixing bowl. In a second medium bowl, whisk together the buttermilk, eggs, and vanilla. Add the wet ingredients to the dry, and mix until thoroughly combined. Whisk in the melted butter. (The batter can be prepared ahead and refrigerated overnight.)

2. Heat an oiled waffle iron. Pour the appropriate amount of batter (according to the size of your waffle iron) onto the hot griddle, and cook until crisped and golden brown to your liking. Transfer the waffle to a serving plate and repeat with the remaining batter.

6 servings

WHIPPED VANILLA BUTTER

One 1-inch piece of vanilla bean

12 tablespoons (1½ sticks) unsalted butter, at room temperature

⅛ teaspoon salt

1. Cut the vanilla bean in half lengthwise and scrape the seeds into a small bowl. Reserve the scraped pod for the Black Pepper Maple Syrup. Add the butter and salt to the bowl, and whip with a handheld electric mixer until light and fluffy.

2. Transfer the butter to a small container, cover, and refrigerate until ready to use.

Generous 12 tablespoons

BLACK PEPPER MAPLE SYRUP

1½ cups grade-A dark amber maple syrup

½ teaspoon freshly ground black pepper

2 tablespoons Crystal hot sauce

One 1-inch scraped vanilla bean pod (from making Whipped Vanilla Butter)

Combine all the ingredients in a small saucepan and bring to a boil. Remove from the heat and allow the flavors to steep until ready to serve. Remove the vanilla bean before serving if desired.

About 1½ cups

EMERIL'S DAY SPRING FARM HERITAGE TURKEY WITH HERBED GRAVY

I had the opportunity to visit Day Spring Farm in Middleburg, Virginia, where farmers Sean and Jessie Baker and their family raise heritage turkeys, Jersey cows, Scottish Highland cattle, Romney sheep, and a variety of heritage chickens, among other things! Heritage turkeys are old breeds that were raised on small farms across the United States and in Europe hundreds of years ago. They were prized for their meat, and some for their plumage. These extraordinary characters live freely on the farm, and are allowed to fly and run around; therefore, they are quite a bit leaner than a commercially grown turkey. In fact, they probably have more in common with their wild cousins. The meat is richer and darker, with a robust turkey flavor. The key to cooking a heritage turkey is keeping it moist. I do this in two ways: First I like to inject the meat with a flavorful solution—sort of a quick brine. Second, I rub butter under the skin, basically making the turkey self-basting. If you have the opportunity to try one of these turkeys, I highly recommend it.

One 10- to 12-pound heritage turkey

For the solution

¼ cup canned low-sodium chicken broth

¼ cup dry white wine

¼ cup olive oil

2 tablespoons freshly squeezed lemon juice

1 tablespoon soy sauce

1 teaspoon cayenne pepper

1 teaspoon salt

For the turkey

3 teaspoons salt

1½ teaspoons freshly ground black pepper

1 medium onion, roughly chopped

1 carrot, roughly chopped

1 celery stalk, roughly chopped

5 sprigs fresh thyme, or ½ teaspoon dried thyme

1 bay leaf

1 lemon, quartered

4 tablespoons (½ stick) unsalted butter, at room temperature

2 tablespoons chopped fresh flat-leaf parsley

1 tablespoon chopped fresh thyme leaves

1 tablespoon chopped fresh sage leaves

2 teaspoons chopped fresh rosemary leaves

2 teaspoons minced garlic

Herbed Gravy (page 264)

1. Place the turkey in the kitchen sink and remove its wrapping. Using your hands, remove the neck, gizzards, heart, and liver—usually found in a small paper or plastic bag inside the cavity. (Reserve for making Turkey Stock, page 265.) Rinse the turkey inside and out under cold running water. Pat it dry inside and out with paper towels.

2. Combine all the ingredients for the solution in a small bowl. Using a turkey injector, inject the solution into the meat of the breast, thigh, back, wings, and legs (see Note). You will have to refill the injector several times. It is best to inject small amounts of solution at regular intervals all over the turkey.

3. Season the inside of the turkey with ½ teaspoon of the salt and ½ teaspoon of the black pepper. Stuff the cavity with the onion, carrot, celery, thyme sprigs, bay leaf, and lemon quarters.

4. Using kitchen twine, tie the ends of the turkey's legs together so that it looks as if it is trying to cross its legs. Season the outside of the turkey all over with 1 teaspoon of the salt and ½ teaspoon of the pepper.

5. Combine the butter, parsley, thyme, sage, rosemary, garlic, remaining 1½ teaspoons salt, and remaining ½ teaspoon black pepper in a bowl, and mix until smooth. Loosen the skin around the turkey breast with your fingers, and carefully insert the butter mixture between the meat and the skin. Rub any leftover butter mixture evenly over the outside of the entire turkey. Fit a roasting rack inside a roasting pan. Place the turkey on the rack, and cover the roasting pan with oiled parchment paper. Refrigerate the turkey for 6 to 8 hours to allow the solution to penetrate throughout the meat.

6. Position a rack in the lower third of the oven and preheat the oven to 450°F.

7. Transfer the turkey to the oven and bake, uncovered, for 15 minutes.

8. Reduce the oven temperature to 350°F and continue to cook for 1 hour, basting occasionally with the pan drippings. If the turkey begins to look too browned, cover the top loosely with aluminum foil until it is done. When the turkey is cooked, the juices will run clear when you insert the tip of a knife at the joint of the leg and thigh. The internal temperature of a heritage turkey should be slightly lower than that of a commercial turkey, from 145° to 150°F.

9. Carefully remove the roasting pan from the oven and cover the turkey loosely with aluminum foil. Let the turkey rest for 20 to 30 minutes before carving. Save the drippings and pan juices to make the gravy.

10. Transfer the turkey to a carving board, and carve. Serve with the Herbed Gravy.

Note: Turkey injectors are available at most kitchen supply stores.

6 servings

HERBED GRAVY

8 tablespoons (1 stick) butter

½ cup all-purpose flour

4 cups Turkey Stock or chicken stock (recipe follows)

1 tablespoon chopped fresh flat-leaf parsley leaves

1 tablespoon chopped fresh sage leaves

1 teaspoon chopped fresh thyme leaves

1 teaspoon chopped fresh rosemary leaves

1 teaspoon salt

½ teaspoon freshly ground black pepper

1 teaspoon cider vinegar (optional)

1. Melt the butter in a heavy 4-quart pot, and stir in the flour. Cook the mixture over moderate heat, whisking as needed, until lightly browned, 5 minutes. Add the stock in a stream, whisking constantly to prevent lumps, and bring to a boil. Reduce the heat to low, stir in any turkey juices accumulated on the platter, and simmer for 5 minutes. Add all the herbs and the salt and pepper. Add the cider vinegar, if desired, and mix well.

2. Remove from the heat and serve immediately, or keep warm until ready to serve.

About 4 cups

TURKEY STOCK

Turkey neck, heart, and gizzard

1 large carrot, roughly chopped

1 onion, roughly chopped

1 large celery stalk, roughly chopped

1 head garlic, cut in half

1 small bay leaf

1 sprig fresh thyme

1 sprig fresh rosemary

4 sprigs fresh parsley

4 cups chicken stock, canned low-sodium chicken broth, or water

4 cups water

1. Combine all the ingredients in a large heavy saucepan and bring to a boil over high heat. Reduce the heat to low and simmer until the stock is reduced to 5 cups, about 1 hour.

2. Strain the stock into a clean pot or large measuring cup, and set it aside.

5 cups

PAN-ROASTED DUCK BREASTS WITH APPLE CIDER REDUCTION

This recipe was developed for domesticated duck. But, hey, if you enjoy the deep flavor of wild duck and have a hunter buddy, you could adapt it by searing the breasts very quickly in the pan over high heat (taking care not to overcook them since wild ducks are typically very lean). You would also need more breasts for this recipe because wild ducks are so much smaller. We love this dish served with the Braised Apples, Roasted Acorn Squash, and Fresh Thyme on page 128.

. . . .

2 cups apple cider or pressed apple juice

2 cups beef stock or canned low-sodium beef broth

1 cinnamon stick (3 inches long)

4 whole cloves

4 black peppercorns

⅔ cup sliced shallot

Two 8-ounce duck breasts, skin scored a few times on the diagonal

½ teaspoon kosher salt

½ teaspoon freshly ground black pepper

1 teaspoon olive oil

1. Combine the apple cider, beef stock, cinnamon stick, cloves, peppercorns, and shallot in a 2-quart saucepan, and bring to a boil over medium-high heat. Reduce the heat so that the liquid just simmers, and cook until the mixture, including the seasoning, has reduced to 1 cup, 35 to 40 minutes. (Have a liquid measure nearby so that you can check the volume as necessary.) Let the sauce cool for a few minutes; then strain it through a fine-mesh sieve into a bowl, discarding the shallot and spices. Set it aside.

2. Season the duck breasts on both sides with the salt and pepper. Heat the olive oil in a 12-inch skillet over medium heat. Add the breasts, skin side down, and cook for 2 minutes. Then reduce the heat to medium-low and cook for 7 minutes longer, or until the skin is golden brown and crisp and most of the fat has been rendered. Carefully drain off most of the fat. Turn the duck breasts, skin side up, raise the heat to medium, and cook for 3 to 4 minutes for medium-rare. Transfer the duck breasts to a cutting board, and allow them to rest for 5 minutes.

3. Drain and discard any remaining fat from the skillet, and set it over medium-high heat. Add the sauce and cook until it has reduced by half or until it is syrupy, about 4 minutes. Remove from the heat.

4. Slice the duck breasts diagonally into ¼-inch-thick slices. Serve with the sauce spooned over the top.

2 to 3 servings

HONEY-BRINED PORK CHOPS WITH NECTARINE CHUTNEY

These brined pork chops are able to stand alone, but if you've already made the chutney (when the nectarines were in season and the getting was good), just grab the jar off the shelf and serve it alongside. Another way to make things simpler: Make the brine for the chops the night before. Then in the morning, before you go to work, just add them to the brine and they'll be ready for cookin' when you get home.

8 cups water

½ cup plus 2 tablespoons kosher salt

2 cups honey

½ bunch fresh thyme, about 6 sprigs

1 tablespoon plus ⅛ teaspoon freshly ground black pepper

1 tablespoon ground cloves

4 bone-in pork chops (about 12 ounces each)

2 tablespoons olive oil

¼ teaspoon salt

Nectarine Chutney (recipe follows), for serving (optional)

1. Pour the water, kosher salt, and honey into a large pot and bring to a boil, stirring to dissolve the salt and honey. Remove from the heat and add the thyme, the 1 tablespoon pepper, and the cloves. Set aside to cool. Then transfer the brine to the refrigerator and chill thoroughly, about 2 hours.

2. Submerge the pork chops in the cold brining liquid and marinate for 6 hours, refrigerated.

3. Remove the pork chops from the brine and pat them dry with paper towels. Discard the brine.

4. Preheat the oven to 350°F.

5. Heat the oil in a large grill pan or heavy skillet over medium-high heat. Season the chops with the ¼ teaspoon salt and the remaining ⅛ teaspoon black pepper. Cook the chops, in batches if necessary, until nicely browned on both sides, about 1 minute per side. Transfer them to a roasting pan or baking sheet, and roast until they reach an internal temperature of 145°F, 10 to 12 minutes. Allow the chops to rest for 5 minutes before serving.

6. Serve each pork chop with a spoonful of the nectarine chutney.

4 servings

NECTARINE CHUTNEY

This chutney is tangy, with a slight sweet note from the nectarines. You could substitute peaches, apricots, or plums in this recipe just as easily. We know it's delicious with the pork, but enjoy this chutney as a condiment on a cheese plate as well.

3 pounds nectarines, pitted and roughly chopped

2 cups cider vinegar

1½ cups thinly sliced red onions

1½ cups packed light brown sugar

1 cup dried cherries

2 cloves garlic, cut in half

2 teaspoons kosher salt

½ teaspoon cayenne pepper

¼ teaspoon ground cloves

¼ teaspoon ground allspice

¼ teaspoon ground cinnamon

1. Combine all the ingredients in a large saucepan, and bring to a boil. Reduce the heat to a slow simmer and cook the chutney for 1 hour, or until most of the liquid has been absorbed.

2. Carefully pour the hot chutney into three sterilized 8-ounce jars, and seal immediately. The chutney should be used within 6 months.

About 3 cups

PORK LOIN WITH A WALNUT AND HERBED FARMER'S CHEESE STUFFING AND PEAR-PARSNIP PUREE

Pork loin roasts are one of my favorite things to cook for family gatherings and impromptu parties. It is a versatile cut of meat that works well for just about any occasion. Stuffing a pork loin not only makes it special but also keeps the roast moist while it is cooking. This stuffing is simple to put together, and can be made ahead of time and kept in the refrigerator until you are ready to use it.

. . . .

½ cup golden raisins (sultanas)

¼ cup walnut liqueur

8 ounces farmer's cheese or other fresh soft cheese (such as quark, queso fresco, or Boursin)

1 teaspoon chopped fresh rosemary leaves

1 teaspoon chopped fresh thyme leaves

1 teaspoon chopped fresh parsley leaves

1 cup chopped toasted walnuts

2 teaspoons salt

One 4-pound boneless pork loin

1 teaspoon freshly ground black pepper

2 teaspoons unsalted butter

¼ cup dry unseasoned bread-crumbs

1. Preheat the oven to 400°F.

2. Combine the raisins and walnut liqueur in a small bowl, and set aside until the raisins are plump, 10 to 15 minutes.

3. Place a small sauté pan over medium-high heat, add the raisins (and any remaining liqueur), and cook for 3 to 5 minutes, or until all the liquid has evaporated from the pan. Transfer the raisins to a bowl. Add the cheese, rosemary, thyme, parsley, walnuts, and ½ teaspoon of the salt, and mix well. If the mixture is too soft, place it in the refrigerator for a few minutes to firm up.

4. To prepare the pork loin for stuffing, first trim off any remaining tough silverskin. Then place the loin on a cutting board, and using a sharp boning knife, slice vertically down the center of the loin without slicing all the way through; leave about an inch of meat to act as a hinge. As you slice the pork, open it with your fingers to form a channel in which to place the stuffing. Pipe or spoon the stuffing into the channel down the center of the loin. Cut eight 18-inch pieces of kitchen twine, and shimmy the twine under the pork at regular intervals. Bring the sides of the pork loin together and tie the roast, enclosing the stuffing. Season the pork loin all over with the remaining 1½ teaspoons salt and the pepper. Place the pork in a roasting pan fitted with a rack.

5. Melt the butter in a small sauté pan, and when it is bubbly, stir in the breadcrumbs. Cook until the breadcrumbs are golden brown, stirring frequently, about 3 minutes. Sprinkle the breadcrumbs evenly over the top of the pork loin.

6. Roast the stuffed pork loin in the oven until an instant-read thermometer inserted into the thickest part of the roast registers 140° to 145°F, usually 35 to 40 minutes. Allow the roast to rest for 10 minutes before slicing.

7. Slice the roast, and serve with the Pear-Parsnip Puree.

8 servings

PEAR-PARSNIP PUREE

Parsnips, a root vegetable closely related to carrots, are considered a winter vegetable because their flavor develops as the temperatures get cooler. I like roasting them to really concentrate their unique sweet, celery-like flavor. The pears, roasted in brown butter and walnut liqueur, add a sweet, nutty taste that complements the parsnips. This is a fall favorite in my house.

1½ pounds parsnips, peeled and chopped

6 tablespoons (¾ stick) unsalted butter

1 tablespoon light brown sugar

¼ teaspoon ground cinnamon

⅛ teaspoon ground allspice

4 ripe Anjou pears, peeled, cored, and cut into 1-inch pieces

2 tablespoons walnut liqueur

½ cup sour cream

½ teaspoon salt

½ teaspoon freshly ground white pepper

1. Preheat the oven to 325°F.

2. Combine the parsnips, 3 tablespoons of the butter, and the brown sugar, cinnamon, and allspice in a small baking dish. Cover the dish tightly with aluminum foil, and bake until the parsnips are tender, about 50 minutes. Remove from the oven and uncover.

3. In a large skillet, melt the remaining 3 tablespoons butter over medium heat. When the butter is just beginning to turn brown, add the pears and cook, stirring, for 3 minutes. Add the liqueur and carefully tilt the pan to ignite the contents. (Alternatively, remove the skillet from the heat, carefully light with a match, and return the skillet to the heat.) Cook while flaming for 2 minutes. Transfer the pears to a food processor.

4. Add the parsnips and any residual juices from the baking dish to the food processor, and puree for 30 seconds. Add the sour cream, salt, and pepper, and process until smooth.

5. Serve immediately, or cover to keep warm until ready to serve.

4 to 6 servings

OUTSTANDING RIB ROAST WITH GREMOLATA

Don't save this for a holiday dinner. Have a get-together tonight so you can have the most amazing roast beef sandwiches tomorrow. Think of it: with the freshest lettuce and tomatoes and a cooled horseradish cream sauce (it'll spread like mayo), cracked black pepper, between slices of toasted bread . . . need I say more?

One 7- to 8-pound beef rib roast (with four rib bones)

¼ cup olive oil

¼ cup smashed garlic cloves (about 10 cloves)

¼ cup canned anchovy fillets

¼ cup chopped onion

½ cup fresh rosemary leaves (from about 5 sprigs)

2 teaspoons kosher salt

2 teaspoons freshly ground black pepper

1 onion, cut into 1-inch pieces

1 carrot, cut into 1-inch pieces

1 celery stalk, cut into 1-inch pieces

1 cup beef or chicken stock, or canned low-sodium beef or chicken broth, as needed

Gremolata (recipe follows)

Fresh Horseradish Cream Sauce (page 186)

1. Tie the roast with cooking twine between the rib bones (in three sections) so it will hold its shape while roasting, and allow it to sit at room temperature for 1 hour.

2. Preheat the oven to 400°F.

3. Place the olive oil, garlic, anchovies, chopped onion, rosemary, salt, and pepper in the bowl of a food processor and process until you have a smooth paste. (Alternatively, chop everything except the oil together, then mash the mixture in a mortar and pestle until smooth; then incorporate the oil.) Set the paste aside.

4. Place the onion, carrot, and celery pieces in a roasting pan or a metal baking dish that is large enough to hold the rib roast. Using a flexible spatula, smear the paste on all sides of the roast. Set the roast on top of the vegetables and roast in the oven for 1½ hours.

5. Continue to cook to desired degree of doneness, checking the internal temperature of the roast with an instant-read thermometer inserted in the thickest part. It should read 125°F to 130°F for rare to medium-rare. If you would prefer the roast to be medium to medium-well throughout, add a cup of broth to the pan to prevent the vegetables from burning, and continue to cook up to 30 minutes longer.

6. Remove the roast from the oven and cut the string. Brush the gremolata over the hot roast, and allow the roast to rest for 30 to 40 minutes so that the juices can redistribute through the meat.

7. To carve the roast, detach the entire section of rib bones by slicing along the side of the roast against the bone until it is separated. Turn the roast on its flat side and slice across the grain to the desired thickness. Alternatively, you can serve the beef without separating the ribs: turn the roast on its end (vertically), and while holding it steady with a carving fork, carve slices by cutting against the grain with a very sharp knife. Or (probably the easiest way to envision slicing), lay the roast on a cutting board, ribs down, and carve by slicing the ribs apart.

8. Serve the sliced roast with warm Fresh Horseradish Cream Sauce.

8 servings

GREMOLATA

Serve this sprinkled over osso buco, braised lamb shanks, or roast beef.

½ cup minced fresh flat-leaf parsley leaves

1 tablespoon plus 1 teaspoon minced garlic

1 tablespoon grated lemon zest

Combine all the ingredients in a small bowl, and stir to blend.

About ½ cup, 6 servings

BRAISED LAMB SHANKS

If you can find it, opt for grass-fed lamb whenever possible—the flavor is unparalleled. These tender shanks create their own rich sauce that just begs to be served over the Creamy Polenta on page 219, the Creamy Stone-Ground Grits on page 223, simple mashed potatoes, or even steamed white rice. Put this together, pop it in the oven one midafternoon, and come back a couple hours later to a veritable feast.

6 lamb shanks (about 12 ounces each)

2¼ teaspoons kosher salt

2¼ teaspoons freshly ground black pepper

¼ cup all-purpose flour

3 tablespoons olive oil

2 cups chopped onions

¾ cup chopped carrots

¾ cup chopped celery

2 tablespoons minced garlic

1 tablespoon finely chopped fresh rosemary leaves

1½ teaspoons chopped fresh thyme leaves

2 tablespoons tomato paste

2 cups dry red wine

One 28-ounce can Italian tomatoes, undrained, crushed with your hands

3 to 4 cups chicken, veal, or lamb stock, or canned low-sodium chicken broth

2 bay leaves

Creamy Polenta (page 219) or Creamy Stone-Ground Grits (page 223), for serving (optional)

Gremolata (page 274) for serving (optional)

1. Preheat the oven to 375°F.

2. Season the lamb shanks on all sides with 2 teaspoons of the kosher salt and 2 teaspoons of the black pepper. Sprinkle the flour over the shanks, and shake them to remove any excess.

3. Add the oil to a Dutch oven that is just large enough to hold the shanks in one layer, and heat it over high heat. Add the shanks and sear until well browned on all sides, about 8 minutes. Transfer the shanks to a platter.

4. Add the onions, carrots, celery, the remaining ¼ teaspoon salt, and the remaining ¼ teaspoon pepper to the Dutch oven, and cook, stirring, until the vegetables are wilted and golden brown around the edges, about 6 minutes. Add the garlic, rosemary, and thyme, and cook, stirring, for 2 minutes. Add the tomato paste and cook, stirring, for 1 minute. Then add the wine and cook, stirring to loosen any brown bits on the bottom and sides of the pan, until the wine has reduced by about half, about 5 minutes.

5. Return the shanks to the pot and add the tomatoes, stock, and bay leaves. Bring to a boil, cover the pot, and place it in the oven. Bake until the shanks are fork-tender, turning them once or twice to ensure even tenderness, 2 to 2½ hours.

6. Remove the pot from the oven and carefully transfer the shanks to a serving platter. Tent the shanks loosely with aluminum foil to keep warm.

7. Remove and discard the bay leaves. Place the Dutch oven over high heat and cook until the braising liquid has reduced to a thick gravy consistency, 5 to 10 minutes.

8. Serve the lamb shanks in wide, shallow bowls, over polenta or grits if desired, with the sauce ladled over the top. Garnish with Gremolata to taste if desired.

6 servings

GRILLED SAUSAGES WITH HOMEMADE MUSTARD

Visit your local butcher, or the sausage maker at your local farmer's market, and select your favorite mix of sausages. Grill 'em up and serve 'em with Emeril's Sauerkraut (page 290) and the Homemade Mustard, and you're in for a real manly-man treat!

5 pounds assorted fresh sausages (seafood, andouille, merguez, Italian, chicken, pork)

½ cup olive oil

Homemade Mustard, for serving (page 278)

1. Preheat the grill to medium-high.

2. Drizzle the sausages with the oil, place them on the grill, and grill for 7 minutes. Then turn them over and cook for another 7 minutes. (Cooking times will vary based on the type of sausage; they are cooked through when the juices run clear when the sausages are pierced with the tip of a knife.)

4 servings

HOMEMADE MUSTARD

Who knew that making your own mustard could be so easy and delicious? Be forewarned: fresh mustard can have a bit more of a kick to it than many store-bought mustards (in a horseradish-y kind of way). This mellows as the mustard ages.

3 tablespoons whole yellow mustard seeds

2½ tablespoons whole brown mustard seeds

⅓ cup dry white wine

⅓ cup white wine vinegar

1 shallot, minced (about 2 tablespoons)

Pinch of ground allspice

1 teaspoon salt

¼ teaspoon freshly ground white pepper

1. Combine all the ingredients in a nonreactive bowl, and refrigerate covered, overnight.

2. Transfer the mustard mixture to a blender, and process until the mustard has the desired texture and thickness; it is equally delicious whether you leave it chunky or smooth. Store in an airtight, nonreactive container in the refrigerator for up to 2 weeks.

¾ **cup**

home economics:
preserving the harvest

General Guidelines for Home Preserving and Processing

The main objective of preserving is to prevent unwanted growth (such as yeast, mold, and bacteria) from ruining the harvested fruit or vegetable so that you can enjoy your favorite foods throughout the seasons. This is especially helpful when you have harvested more than you know what to do with. If you have ever been fortunate enough to be in this situation, then preserving is for you. Before getting started, though, it is extremely important to read these guidelines on washing, sterilizing, filling, and processing jars. We have assembled a few basic tips for you here, but if you really want to get into canning and preserving, we recommend that you invest in a detailed canning and preserving manual. There are several wonderful such guides available; we personally love the one put out by the Ball canning company. It is an extraordinarily detailed reference, very helpful to have on hand.

Washing the jars

Make sure the jars are in perfect condition—no cracks or chips. Select the size jars you need for your project. You may need half-pint, pint, or quart size, depending on what you're making. You may need wide-mouth (for large things such as whole beets) or narrow-mouth (for something like chutney).

Make sure the lids and bands fit and are not corroded. Wash the jars and lids in hot, soapy water, rinse them thoroughly with hot water, and leave them out to air-dry on clean kitchen towels. If you are going to be heat processing your preserves for storage, do not use lids that have been used before.

Sterilizing the jars

Oven method

Preheat the oven to 225°F. Place folded towels on a baking sheet to create a cushion. Lay the washed jars on their sides on the towels, and shortly before you plan to fill them, heat the jars in the oven for at least 30 minutes.

Bring a small saucepan of water to a simmer, and then remove it from the heat. Drop in the jar lids, cover the pan, and let the lids warm for at least 10 minutes. The lids should not be removed until you are ready to close the jars. It is best, and certainly easiest, to use a magnetic lid lifter to retrieve the lids from the hot water.

Boiling method

Set a rack in a large pot and fill the pot with hot water. Using tongs or a jar lifter, place four clean jars on the rack, filling the jars with water and spacing them 1 inch apart. There should be 1 to 2 inches of water covering the jars. Cover the pot with a lid, bring the water to a boil over high heat, and boil the jars for 10 minutes. Turn off the heat. Remove the sterilized jars from the hot water and set them upside down on a clean paper towel to drain briefly.

Bring a small saucepan of water to a simmer, and then remove it from the heat. Drop in the jar lids, cover the pan, and let the lids warm for at least 10 minutes. The lids should not be removed until you are ready to close the jars. It is best, and certainly easiest, to use a magnetic lid lifter to retrieve the lids from the hot water.

At this point, the jars and lids are sterilized. Now follow the particular recipe directions precisely, because the processing methods vary from one recipe to the next. For instance, some recipes require heat processing after the jars have been filled. Other recipes are for foods that do not require heat processing, and can be stored for shorter lengths of time.

Filling the jars

Turn the sterilized jars right side up. Pack the pickling/preserving ingredients/mixture in the jars. This is best done using a canning funnel—it helps keep the tops of the jars clean, which is extremely important in ensuring a proper seal later. Ladle the hot brine (if pickling) into the jars, leaving a ½-inch headspace. Sweet mixtures that are not acidic, such as jams and jellies, usually require a ¼-inch headspace. Wipe the rims clean with a damp paper towel, affix the lids, seal with the rings, and tighten. When filling the jars with hot liquids, the lids will seal (pop) as the jars and their contents cools. If you are not processing, refrigerate the jars once they have cooled. Generally jars that have not been heat processed will have a 4- to 6-month shelf life.

Processing the ingredients

Using the jar lifter, return the filled and sealed jars to the pot of hot water that you used to sterilize the jars. There should be 1 to 2 inches of water to cover the jars. Cover the pot with a lid, bring the water to a gentle boil, and process for the length of time indicated in the recipe, usually between 10 and 15 minutes. Carefully remove the jars and set them aside to cool in a dark place. The lids will "pop" as the jars cool. Any jars whose lids do not seal properly should be refrigerated once cool and then enjoyed within 2 weeks. The shelf life for unopened processed jars is typically 1 year if stored in a cool, dark place. (Refrigerate the jars promptly after opening.)

GREEN TOMATO PICCALILLI

This tomato relish is one way to enjoy green tomatoes year-round. Spoon it over hot dogs, use it as a garnish for red beans and rice or baked beans, or serve it as a condiment on a cheese plate.

3 pounds green tomatoes, cored and cut into ½-inch dice

4 medium onions, chopped

¼ cup kosher salt

2 red bell peppers, seeded and finely chopped

1½ cups packed light brown sugar

½ cup granulated sugar

2 cups distilled white vinegar

1 cup cider vinegar

2 cinnamon sticks (3 inches each)

1 tablespoon whole yellow mustard seeds

1 teaspoon ground allspice

½ teaspoon crushed red pepper

¼ teaspoon ground cloves

1. In a large glass bowl, or other nonreactive container, layer the diced tomatoes and the onions, sprinkling the kosher salt between the layers. You should have used all of the salt by the time you have finished layering the tomatoes and onions. Cover with plastic wrap and refrigerate overnight.

2. Drain the tomatoes and onions, and rinse them briefly under cool running water. Place them in a large enameled or other nonreactive saucepan, add all the remaining ingredients, and bring to a boil. Reduce the heat to low and simmer until the vegetables are very tender, about 30 minutes.

3. Remove the pan from the heat and discard the cinnamon sticks. Spoon the relish into hot sterilized jars, and attach the lids and rings. Process the jars in a hot water bath for 10 minutes. Remove them from the hot water bath and set them aside to cool.

4. Store the jars in a cool, dark place for up to 1 year. (Any jars that do not seal should be refrigerated promptly and the piccalilli enjoyed within 2 months.)

2½ quarts

SPICY TOMATO JAM

This spicy jam is the perfect thing to make in the deep of summer when everyone has ripe tomatoes to spare. It's great with grilled chicken or pork, and is also nice alongside cheese and crackers. Or try a dollop with crispy fried oysters or on top of a simple grilled burger.... It's very intensely flavored—a little goes a long way.

4 cups peeled, seeded, and chopped ripe tomatoes (2½ to 3 pounds tomatoes)

2 lemons, peel cut entirely away and discarded, seeds removed, flesh finely chopped

1½ cups sugar

2 tablespoons minced fresh ginger

½ teaspoon crushed red pepper

2 pinches salt

1. Combine all the ingredients in a medium saucepan and bring to a boil. Lower the heat to a brisk simmer and continue to cook, periodically skimming off any foam that forms on the surface and stirring frequently, until a thick, jamlike consistency is achieved and most of the liquid has evaporated, 30 to 35 minutes. (Stir more frequently during the last 10 minutes so the jam does not burn on the bottom of the pan.)

2. Transfer the jam to hot sterilized jars, filling the jars to within ½ inch from the top, and attach the lids and rings.

3. Once they have cooled, store the jars in the refrigerator for up to 4 months. (Alternatively, place the jam in covered nonreactive containers and store in the refrigerator for up to 2 weeks.)

1 generous pint, two 8-ounce jars

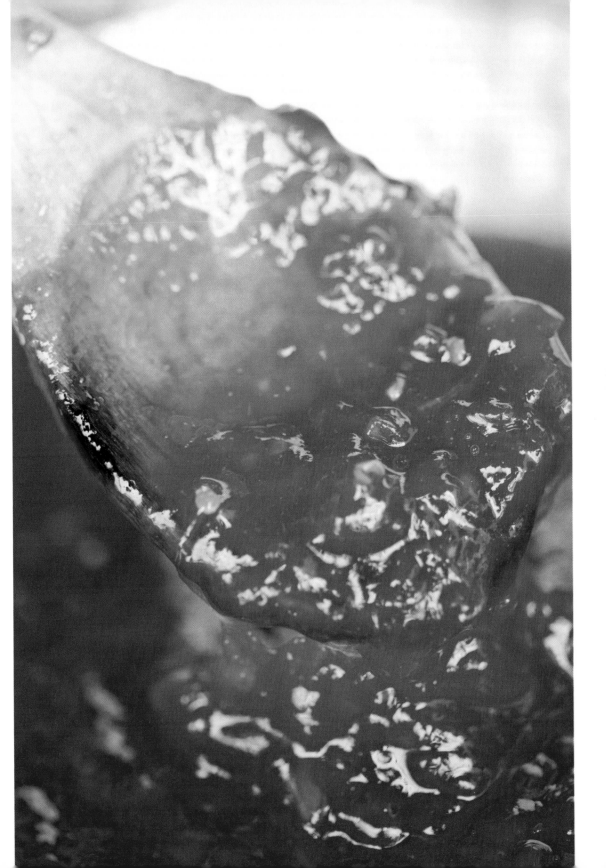

HOMEMADE HOT SAUCE

This recipe can be modified to use whatever type of chiles you like. The flavor, and the heat level, will vary greatly depending on the chiles you use. Talk about kickin' it up a notch—how you want to do it depends on you! Made with red Fresno peppers, the sauce is piquant with a full-bodied richness. Made with the jalapeños, it is very spicy, yet still full of depth. Many times the fieriness of the sauce will depend not only on the species of pepper but on the peppers themselves. If you are adventurous, just go for it: taste, and decide on your favorite for yourself. If you want a mild chile sauce, remove some or all of the seeds from the peppers before proceeding.

2 teaspoons vegetable oil

10 ounces fresh red Fresno chiles or jalapeños, stemmed and cut crosswise into ½-inch-thick slices (see Note)

6 cloves garlic, smashed

¾ cup thinly sliced onions

¾ cup chopped carrots

1¾ teaspoons salt

2 cups water

¼ cup chopped fresh cilantro leaves and stems

1 cup distilled white vinegar

1. Heat the oil in a small saucepan over high heat. Add the chiles, garlic, onions, and carrots. Add the salt. Cook the peppers in the pan for 5 minutes; it is okay if they blister or blacken, stirring as needed.

2. Add the water and cilantro, and reduce the heat to medium-high. Cook for 20 minutes, or until the peppers are soft and almost all of the liquid has evaporated. (Note: This should be done in a very well ventilated area!) Remove the pan from the heat and allow the peppers to cool to room temperature.

3. Transfer the mixture to a food processor or blender, and puree for 15 seconds. While the machine is still running, add the vinegar in a steady stream, continuing to puree on high speed until smooth, about 1 minute. Transfer the sauce to a sterilized pint jar, bottles, or other container. Cover and refrigerate for up to 6 months.

Note: If you are a fan of poblano peppers, substitute 6 ounces roasted poblanos (about 2 peppers) and 6 ounces jalapeños for the 10 ounces of chiles above. (See page 44 for roasting instructions.)

About 2 cups

WATERMELON RIND CRISP SWEET PICKLES

This is a delightfully sweet treat, hitting all of your taste buds and playing your palate with different spice notes. You'll have plenty of watermelon rind from the summer months, so why not give it a try?

6 cups cold water

⅓ cup pickling salt

6 cups peeled watermelon rind (white and light pink part only), cut into ¾-inch cubes

2 cups ice cubes

4½ cups sugar

2 cups distilled white vinegar

2 cups water

4 cinnamon sticks (3 inches each)

2 bay leaves

1 tablespoon whole yellow mustard seeds

1 tablespoon whole coriander seeds

1½ teaspoon whole allspice berries

½ teaspoon whole cloves

1. In a large bowl, whisk together the cold water and pickling salt. Place the watermelon rind in another large nonreactive mixing bowl, and pour the salt-water mixture over it. Add the ice cubes, transfer to the refrigerator, and let sit for at least 6 hours or overnight.

2. Drain the watermelon rind and rinse it thoroughly under cold running water. Transfer it to a large pot, cover with water, and bring to a boil. Reduce the heat to a simmer and cook until fork-tender, 10 to 15 minutes. Do not overcook. Drain, and set aside.

3. Combine all the remaining ingredients in a large pot, and bring to a boil. Reduce the heat to a low simmer and cook for 10 minutes. Then add the drained watermelon rind and cook for about 1 hour, or until the rind is almost completely translucent.

4. Divide the watermelon rind between two sterilized pint canning jars, and add enough pickling liquid to cover the rind by at least ¼ inch. Add a cinnamon stick to each jar. There should be at least ½-inch headspace. Wipe the rims clean with a damp paper towel, and attach the lids and rings. Process the jars in a hot water bath for 10 minutes.

5. Remove the jars from the hot water and let them cool. The jars should seal as they cool. Any jar that does not seal properly should be refrigerated and the pickles consumed within 2 weeks.

6. Watermelon pickles will keep, stored in a cool dark place, for up to 1 year.

2 pints

EMERIL'S SAUERKRAUT

When there's cabbage, make sauerkraut. Of course it's fresher and more flavorful if you do it yourself! You'll never buy it again. It's easy: shred the cabbage, salt it, press it, and allow it to ferment in a cool dark place. That's it. A natural preserving process ensues. What's important is that you place enough weight on top of the cabbage so that it exudes enough liquid to cover.

5 pounds cabbage, cored and shredded

5 tablespoons kosher salt

1½ cups thinly sliced red onion (about half an onion)

4 cloves garlic, thinly sliced (about ¼ cup)

2 jalapeños, thinly sliced (about ½ cup)

1. In a 6-quart enameled pot or other nonreactive container, such as a crock or a large glass container, layer the ingredients: cabbage, salt, onion, garlic, and jalapeño. Repeat this three or four more times, ending with a layer of cabbage and salt. Press it with your hands. The salt will begin to extract juices from the cabbage, and it will wilt. After a few minutes, all of the cabbage will fit. Place a piece of cheesecloth over the top, invert a plate or other flat surface on top of the cheesecloth, and press it down again.

2. Weight the cabbage with a 5-pound brick wrapped in plastic wrap or with another heavy object set over the plate. Once the cabbage has shrunk enough, cover the container. Allow the cabbage to sit in a cool place (65° to 70°F) for 2 to 3 days to begin fermentation.

3. Check the cabbage. There should be enough liquid to cover. It should smell wonderfully aromatic and be absent of any browned shreds. Leave the cabbage to ferment further, for a total time of 2 weeks.

4. Transfer the sauerkraut and its juices to sterilized pint jars or other containers, attach the lids and rings, and refrigerate for up to 6 weeks.

4 pints

SPICY PICKLED OKRA

In Louisiana, many folks enjoy pickled okra on relish trays and as garnishes for their favorite cocktails. This tasty snack makes a mean stirrer for a spicy bloody mary or martini! Try to get young, small okra, since they will be very tender and will also fit nicely into the canning jars.

2 pounds fresh young okra
(2- to 3-inch pods)

Ice water

5 cups distilled white vinegar

6 tablespoons kosher salt

8 cloves garlic

16 fresh hot peppers, such as
Tabasco or Serrano

¼ cup whole yellow mustard seeds

1. Wash the okra under cold running water. Trim the stem ends, leaving at least ⅓ inch of the cap intact. Soak the okra in ice water to cover for 1 hour.

2. Drain the okra and pat it dry. Divide the okra among four or five sterilized pint canning jars, inserting the okra cap side down.

3. Bring the vinegar, salt, garlic, hot peppers, and mustard seeds to a boil in a large nonreactive pot. Reduce the heat and simmer for 5 minutes.

4. Divide the peppers, garlic cloves, and mustard seeds evenly among the jars of okra. Cover with the hot pickling liquid by at least ¼ inch, leaving at least ½ inch of headspace. Make sure there are no air bubbles in the jars, wipe the rims clean, and attach the lids and rings. Process the jars in a hot water bath for 10 minutes.

5. Remove the jars from the hot water and let them cool. The jars should seal as they cool. Store the jars in a cool, dark place for up to 1 year. (Any jars that do not vacuum-seal properly should be refrigerated and the pickles consumed within 2 weeks.) Allow the pickles to mature for at least 4 weeks before consuming.

Four or five 1-pint jars

PICKLED GREEN BEANS

When there's an abundance of fresh green beans in the market or in the garden, pickle 'em. If you have a dried hot pepper, go ahead, live a little, and stick it in the jar too.

3½ cups water

1½ cups white wine vinegar

2 tablespoons pickling salt

2 tablespoon sugar

½ teaspoon crushed red pepper

1¾ pounds fresh green beans, rinsed, patted dry, and trimmed to fit in the jars

½ cup thinly sliced sweet onion, such as Texas 1015 or Vidalia

4 cloves garlic, smashed

1. Combine the water, vinegar, salt, sugar, and crushed red pepper in a small saucepan, and bring to a boil. Reduce the heat to low and simmer for 2 minutes.

2. Pack the beans, onion, and garlic evenly in four sterilized pint jars. Ladle the hot brine into the jars, leaving ½ inch of headspace. Wipe the rims of the jars clean with a damp paper towel, and attach the lids and rings. Process the jars in a hot water bath for 15 minutes.

3. Carefully remove the jars and set them in a cool, dark place for up to 1 year. Allow 2 weeks before opening. (Any jars that do not seal properly should be promptly refrigerated and the beans consumed within 1 month.)

4 pints

KOSHER-STYLE DILL PICKLES

Cold and crispy garlicky pickle slices made from farm-fresh cucumbers.

....

1½ pounds fresh pickling
   cucumbers, such as Kirby

6 sprigs fresh dill

3 cups water

1 cup distilled white vinegar

2 tablespoons kosher salt

9 cloves garlic, smashed

2 bay leaves, crumbled

1 teaspoon dried dill weed or dill
   seeds

½ teaspoon black peppercorns

½ teaspoon whole fennel seeds

1. Trim off the stem ends of the cucumbers, and slice them into ¼-inch-thick rounds. Divide the cucumber slices evenly among three pint jars or other nonreactive containers of similar size. Add 2 dill sprigs to each container.

2. Combine all the remaining ingredients in a small saucepan, and bring to a boil. Then reduce the heat to a simmer and cook for 5 minutes.

3. Ladle the hot brine over the cucumbers, being sure to get 3 cloves of garlic into each container. Set the jars aside, uncovered, to cool for 1 hour at room temperature. Refrigerate the jars for 1 hour. Then cover and store in the refrigerator for up to 3 months.

3 pints

PORTUGUESE PICKLED ONIONS

This recipe is inspired by the little onions jarred by my good friends over at Star Pickling in Swansea, Massachusetts. Couldn't get their secret recipe, but that doesn't keep me from making 'em. These are next best!

2½ pounds very small boiling onions, soaked in hot water for 10 minutes (for easier peeling) and peeled

2½ cups water

2½ cups distilled white vinegar

2½ tablespoons pickling salt

2½ tablespoons sugar

2 tablespoons whole yellow mustard seeds

1¾ teaspoons crushed red pepper

15 medium bay leaves

1. Bring a small pot of salted water to a boil over high heat. Add the peeled onions, remove the pot from the heat, and let steep for 3 minutes. Drain, and set the onions aside.

2. In another small pot, combine the water, vinegar, salt, sugar, mustard seeds, crushed red pepper, and bay leaves. Bring to a boil. Then reduce the heat to low and simmer for 10 minutes.

3. Divide the onions evenly among four sterilized wide-mouth pint jars. Ladle the hot brine into the jars, dividing the bay leaves evenly, leaving ½ inch of headspace. Wipe the rims clean with a damp paper towel, and attach the lids and rings. Process the jars in a hot water bath for 10 minutes.

4. Carefully remove the jars and set them in a cool, dark place for up to 1 year. Allow at least 5 days before serving.

4 pints

HERBED OIL

Do it yourself instead of buying herbed oils. It'll be better. It'll be fresher. Drizzle over everything. Make gifts for everyone.

. . . .

1 quart McEvoy Ranch Traditional Blend olive oil or other good-quality olive oil

1 bunch (about 5 sprigs) fresh rosemary

2 sprigs fresh oregano

2 sprigs fresh thyme

¼ teaspoon crushed red pepper

1. Combine all the ingredients in a medium saucepan, and bring to a simmer. Immediately remove the pan from the heat and allow the herbs and spices to steep in the hot oil for 20 minutes.

2. Strain the oil or leave the herbs and spices in it, and store it in clean glass bottles. Use within 1 month.

1 quart

FIGS IN SYRUP

This is a terrific way of extending the short fig season. Put away a few jars and then enjoy eating these glistening beauties over hot buttered biscuits for a real taste of summer long after it's gone.

2½ pounds (about 8 cups)
    firm-ripe figs

4 cups sugar

1 cup water

1 vanilla bean, halved, seeds
    scraped out and reserved

1 lemon, halved

1. Trim the tips of the fig stems if they are long. Rinse the figs under cool running water, and transfer them to a large nonreactive pot. Add the sugar, water, vanilla bean halves and seeds, and the juice of one lemon half. Cook over low heat, stirring gently occasionally, until the sugar has dissolved. Raise the heat to medium and bring the syrup to a boil. Then reduce the heat and cook at a low boil for 10 minutes. Remove the pot from the heat. Slice the remaining lemon half into thin slices, and gently stir them into the figs. Cover the pot and let it sit overnight.

2. Remove the lid, set the pot over medium-high heat, and bring to a boil. Then remove it from the heat, and using a slotted spoon, transfer the figs, including the vanilla bean halves and the lemon slices, to sterilized jars. Add enough of the hot syrup to cover the figs, leaving ½ inch of headspace. Wipe the rims of the jars clean with a wet paper towel, and attach the lids and rings. Set the jars aside in a cool, dark place. The jars will seal as they cool. These will keep for up to 6 months.

About 3 pints

PICKLED BEETS

Enjoy these straight out of the jar, slice them for a nice salad, or quarter and serve them on their own as a side dish. Many of you remember a treat such as these from your grandmother's table. Bring them to your own. Delicious.

. . . .

2 cups cider vinegar

½ cup sugar

½ cup water

2 teaspoons pickling salt

2 teaspoons whole coriander seeds

2 teaspoons whole yellow mustard seeds

3 whole cardamom pods

2 whole cloves

One 1-inch piece of fresh ginger, peeled and roughly chopped

10 medium beets (about 2 pounds), roasted (see page 172), peeled, and quartered

1. Combine all the ingredients except the beets in a medium saucepan, and heat to a simmer. Lower the heat and cook for 3 minutes, or until the sugar has completely dissolved.

2. Divide the beets evenly between two sterilized pint jars. Ladle the hot brine into the jars, leaving ½ inch of headspace. Wipe the rims clean with a damp paper towel, and attach the lids and rings. Process the jars in a hot water bath for 15 minutes.

3. Carefully remove the jars and set them in a cool, dark place for up to 1 year. Allow 3 weeks before opening. (Any jars that do not seal properly should be promptly refrigerated and the beets consumed within 1 month.)

2 pints

BRANDIED CHERRIES

A "for grown-ups only" fruit cocktail—don't pack these in the lunch box! Eat them like candy, serve them over ice cream, or use them as a garnish for chocolate desserts. These cherries would also make a killer cake filling if finely chopped and then spread between cake layers.

1½ pounds ripe cherries, stemmed and pitted

1 cup sugar, or a bit more to taste

1 cup brandy, or more as needed

1. Layer the cherries with the sugar in a sterilized quart-size canning jar or other nonreactive lidded container. Slowly pour the brandy over all, adding it little by little as the sugar absorbs the liquid. Cover the jar and shake gently to distribute the sugar. Add more brandy if needed to cover the cherries. Set the jar aside in a cool, dark place for 6 weeks, shaking it occasionally to dissolve the sugar and checking the brandy level periodically; add more brandy if necessary to keep the cherries covered.

2. The cherries should be ready in 6 weeks but will continue to improve in flavor for up to 1 year. Store in the refrigerator.

1 quart

PEACH FREEZER JAM

If you want to preserve the fresh fruit of summer but don't feel like standing over a hot stove and sterilizing jars, this quick, foolproof method is for you. Just make sure that you follow the directions as outlined below, and measure the fruit and sugar precisely to ensure a good set on the jam.

2¾ cups finely chopped peeled and pitted ripe peaches (about 2¼ pounds)

6½ cups sugar

2 pouches (1 box) Certo liquid fruit pectin (6 ounces total)

⅓ cup freshly squeezed lemon juice

¼ teaspoon almond extract

1 vanilla bean, halved, seeds scraped out and reserved, bean cut into 8 small pieces

1. Combine the peaches and sugar in a large mixing bowl, and stir to combine. Set aside for 10 minutes, stirring occasionally. The sugar should be nearly dissolved.

2. In a separate bowl, combine the pectin and lemon juice.

3. Stir the pectin mixture into the peach-sugar mixture, and stir constantly until the sugar is no longer grainy and is nearly completely dissolved, about 3 minutes. Add the almond extract and the vanilla seeds, and stir to combine. Spoon the jam into clean ½-pint or pint jars. Place 1 or 2 pieces of vanilla bean inside each jar. Cover the jars and let stand at room temperature until the jam is set, up to 24 hours.

4. Store the jam in the refrigerator for up to 3 weeks, or in the freezer for up to 1 year. Defrost the jam in the fridge before serving.

Eight ½-pint or four 1-pint jars

HOMEMADE APPLESAUCE

Make this simple classic when apples are at their peak and you'll be amazed at how delicious applesauce really can be. I find that the best results come from using a mixture of tart and sweet apples, and I always try to use a red-skinned variety for at least part of the mix so that the sauce ends up a beautiful rosy hue. You could easily serve this warm as a side dish with grilled or roast pork.

5 pounds apples, preferably a mix of tart/sweet and green/red

1 cup apple cider

2 cinnamon sticks (3 inches each)

1 teaspoon whole allspice berries

¼ teaspoon freshly grated nutmeg

3 to 6 tablespoons sugar or light brown sugar, to taste

¼ cup Calvados or brandy (optional)

1. Peel any green apples, and remove the cores and seeds; cut each apple into 8 pieces. Core and remove the seeds from any red apples (do not peel red apples; cooking with the peel on will impart a beautiful rosy color to your applesauce), and cut each apple into 8 pieces.

2. Place all of the apples in a large, heavy saucepan, and add the cider, cinnamon sticks, allspice, and nutmeg. Cover, and bring to a boil over medium-high heat, stirring occasionally. Cook for 30 minutes.

3. Reduce the heat to medium-low and continue to cook, covered and stirring frequently, until the apples have completely broken down into a thick sauce, about 30 minutes. Add the sugar to taste, and the Calvados if desired, and cook for 10 minutes longer.

4. Pass the applesauce through a food mill or a coarse sieve to remove any remaining skins and solids (discard the solids). Set the sauce aside to cool, or enjoy it warm. Store covered in the refrigerator for up to 1 week.

5 cups

Index

Note: Page references in *italics* refer to photographs.

C